KORYEAH
DWANYEN

# UNDERCOVER
# HEARTBREAK

## A MEMOIR OF TRUST & TRAUMA

Undercover Heartbreak: A Memoir of Trust & Trauma

Copyright © Koryeah Dwanyen 2024

ISBN (Softcover) 979-8-35097-565-9

Cover design by: Justin Bābak Hickman

For all the yesterdays that led me to today. . .
My three heartbeats, and my mama. I'm grown now, so you are one
of my lil' friends.

This book is based on a true story. Some names, locations, and identifying characteristics have been changed to protect the privacy of those depicted. Dialogue has been re-created from memory.

# CONTENTS

# MARTHA'S VINEYARD

The flight from Minneapolis to JFK was uneventful, but arriving at my connecting gate, I felt a wave of peace and euphoria. I hadn't anticipated the sea of beautiful Black faces—young, old, and everywhere in between. There were comfy-cute folks and those wearing Louis Vuitton, dressed to the nines, all standing at the same gate. As we waited to board, the gate felt like I was returning to the motherland, Africa, rather than a girls' weekend at Martha's Vineyard with friends from my college days. I couldn't wipe the grin off my face.

There was an immediate sense of community while waiting at the gate. People were chatting, and it reminded me of back when we traveled without phones. We learned about the people around us; some even created friendships while waiting for the plane. I met a woman who was with her husband and daughter. When I shared that this would be my first time visiting, she and her husband told me they'd been coming to the Vineyard from Brooklyn for years and agreed that I would enjoy myself. The more we talked, the more eager I became.

1

Stepping off the airplane felt like stepping into an oven on warm. The sweltering heat enveloped me as I made my way to the baggage claim. The baggage claim area was a small, crowded throwback, but everyone was polite and patient as we waited for space to grab our belongings. It felt like I had taken a step back in time—the airport reminded me of a vacation house, with Adirondack chairs, a playground, and no carousel for baggage claim, just a sign in a small area inside the hall. Despite the delay, people were all smiles.

I finally retrieved my petal pink Away bag and hopped in a cab. I gave the cabbie the address to our Airbnb. Without GPS, he headed for the house and shared history about the island as he drove. He'd lived there his entire life, though as he got older, he split his time between Martha's Vineyard and Cabo.

"Well, you know, I had dreams of buying a house for me and the missus one day. We were saving, but with the outsiders buying property here, well, and all these Airbnbs..."

There was a short silence. I felt a little awkward about contributing to the vacation rental market. But then he continued sharing, and I could feel his pride as he pointed out the historical markers as we passed them.

"Well now, do you know Oak Bluffs?"

"No, tell me."

"Oak Bluffs is known as the welcoming spot for Black folks because, back in the day, it was the only town on the island that let us stay at the local hotels. There's so much history, from the underground railroad to the Inkwell." He slowed the car at a stop sign. "Inkwell, a name given by white folks, you know, but we adopted it as a badge of pride."

"Inkwell," I repeated, looking out the window and picturing decades past, so much changed yet so much still the same.

"Yes, and the Polar Bears was the only safe place for Black swimmers."

At the Airbnb, I was the first of my friends to arrive. I stepped out of the car to find a beautiful white and gray Victorian-style home with a wraparound porch with light blue, pink, foam green, and lavender accents. There were six rocking chairs on the porch that looked ideal for lounging or having a quick cup of coffee, which caught my eye because the woman at the airport had told me that porch life is a cultural must on the Vineyard.

I headed inside to unpack and anxiously awaited everyone else's arrival. I settled into a bedroom, unpacking my suitcase and toiletries into the dresser. I sank into a soft loveseat in the corner of the bedroom and put up my tired feet. It had been a while since I'd had much quiet to stop and think about my life. My brain ticked through the categories.

My job as a tech consultant was pretty good. My days were typically filled with call after call, preparing presentations, traveling to my customers, or attending conferences. I was proud of my income and what I'd accomplished professionally, climbing the ranks and achieving success at every step. I thrived with the fast-paced work, but I also traveled a lot for my job, which was a bit hard with the kids.

The kids. I tapped into my phone gallery to swipe through my gallery of favorite pictures. I smiled at the picture of my oldest daughter in a soccer game action shot, the picture of my twin boys, sweaty and grinning after flag football practice, and the video my mom had taken of me screaming at the game last Saturday, to the other parents' annoyance.

My ex and I were finally in a pretty good place with co-parenting with minimal conflict. I'd finally found a good therapist, too. I'd been doing a bunch of hard work with her, shadow work, processing failed relationships and childhood traumas. I'd recently celebrated my fortieth birthday with a huge party. I wore a gorgeous white dress and called it my wedding to myself. Maybe it was a little extra, but it symbolized the covenant I made with and for myself. I smiled remembering how beautiful and grounded I'd felt in my flowing white gown. I was moving in a good direction, and it felt good.

ॐ

My friends trickled in over the next couple hours. Phones buzzed as friends joined us, and soon, our gathering was in full swing. Our house's location couldn't have been better situated, right at the intersection of Narragansett and Circuit. It was a prime location for people-watching and neighborly chats.

Even though it had been years since our last reunion, gathering again felt like revisiting my college years. This time, though, we were equipped with a wealth of knowledge and wisdom, and a little more money. Our jokes and playfulness with each other felt so familiar and comfortable. My girls and I lived it up that week, going to comedy shows and the different bars along Circuit Avenue. We danced, ate, rode bikes, bowled, and ate some more, packing each day with adventures, pleasures, and novelty. We even rented a yacht and spent the day on the water. There was squawking and shrieking about the possibility of sharks being in the water, and someone sent an article about local sharks to the group text chat. After panicked vows not to get in the water, a few glasses of wine emboldened us.

The slower pace was exactly what I needed. I used the time to stay in the present. My friends were always eager to jump into conversations that wandered from memory to memory. We vented, joked, and reverted to our twenties with antics and entertainment. While relaxing on the porch, we spotted local wildlife, including skunks that frequented the streets at dusk. We named the main one that kept coming back Charlie. Thankfully, Charlie wasn't scared enough to spray.

Martha's Vineyard felt like an experience everyone should try at least once. Its history, beauty, and old-town charm felt novel but familiar in a healing way—especially Oak Bluffs, which felt like a Black freedom colony. I was spiritually rejuvenated. As a single mother of three children with an active career, it was so rare to have moments dictated only by desire, not obligation or responsibility, and I soaked it all in. It allowed me to sit with my thoughts or, even better, have no thoughts at all. The opportunity to be me, not a mother, sister, daughter, or ex-wife—a version of myself that I couldn't live daily. As I fell asleep on the second-to-last night, I smiled in the dark, happy that I had chosen to take some me time before autumn set in and it was time for the kids' first day of school.

CB

On the last full day of my trip, there was a Florida A&M alum reception at Garde East, a restaurant on the Vineyard. We walked into the lavishly decorated reception hall and found our seats. We were laughing and joking around, continuing to have a good time, when a swarm of men in suits walked into the reception area.

As I focused my attention, I recognized them as Secret Service agents. Barack, Michelle Obama, and several celebrities soon entered the room. Monique, a friend who had been hired to photograph the reception, busily captured moment after moment. After the Obamas had settled, she approached me.

"Coco, would you do me a favor?"

"What?" I replied.

"Will you ask that Secret Service agent if I can take a picture of Barack or get a picture with him?"

Monique was shy and introverted and had a beautiful eye for stills. It was a working vacation for her while the rest of us were laughing it up, enjoying the time together. I knew exactly why she had asked me, but I wanted to hear her explanation anyway.

"Girl, why can't you ask him?" I had already had a glass or two of rosé by that point.

"What if he says no? I'm gonna run away crying. I can't talk to him," she admitted. "But if he tries to say no to you, you won't take no for an answer."

"Okay, I'll do it." I finished the last drop of wine in my glass and walked over to the man.

We made quick pleasantries. I gave him a once-over as he spoke. He was a tall, handsome, lighter-skinned brother, and the way his good looks drew me in distracted me from the purpose of the conversation. My goal got muddled, and I was ready to abort the mission and just flirt. I looked back, saw Monique waiting for a response, and was brought back to my original question.

"Well, I have a job to do," I said abruptly.

"What's that?" he asked, flashing a beautiful white smile.

I returned a prize-winning smile of my own. "My girlfriend is taking pictures and wants to know if she can..."

"I don't know," he interjected with a sterner look. He seemed more interested in having a conversation with me than my request. "They have a tight schedule," he continued, but I had become distracted by his physique.

"It's no big deal," I said, raising an eyebrow. I was taking him all in like a decadent dessert.

He noticed. "What's your name?"

I could see him checking me out in return. "Coco. What's yours?" Continuing to drink him in, I was not disappointed by any angle. I was becoming more attracted by the second.

We both stood awkwardly, with Kool-Aid smiles on our faces for a few seconds.

He shifted his stance and said, "Dale. Where are you from?"

"Detroit."

"Oh, shit," he blurted.

"Why, where are you from?" I asked.

"I'm from the D!"

We did the natural thing that Detroiters do—rep where we're from, the East Side or West Side.

"I'm an East Side girl." I said my line first.

"Oh, hell."

"You must be from the West Side," I said.

"You know it."

Our conversation flowed so naturally. I grabbed his left hand to check out his ring finger. One of my friends called my name, and he pulled his hand back.

"What are you doing?"

I admitted that I was looking for an indentation or a tan line on his finger. "Mm, I was digging the vibe and didn't want to get my hopes up."

"I would tell you something like that," he tried to reassure me.

"History's proven that is, in fact, not true." I'd met many men who didn't care one way or another if they were married, including my ex, Clyde. Some males preyed the moment they were out of the sight of their wives.

"This isn't Maury Povich, you know," he said.

"My life's been a little Maury Povich, sorry to say."

At that, he laughed heartily. "Well, *we* have to get going." He signaled to himself and his entourage of agents.

"Yeah, I know. You guys are going to the film festival."

"How do you know?"

"My girlfriend's volunteering there, so that's why she wanted to get the pictures before she had to leave."

Dale directed me to someone to arrange for the photos to be taken so I could complete my mission. I thanked him and popped back over to tell Monique where we were headed.

As we walked over, a colleague interrupted Dale, and he left without explanation. I realized that Dale was leaving, and we would probably never be able to speak again if we didn't exchange contact information. It was rare to find someone to share with so easily and freely. I felt my anxiety rising—I had to do something to get his attention.

"Dale!" I yelled at the top of my lungs. "Add me on Facebook."

There I was in an atrium filled with two hundred people focused on the Obamas, and I broke the sound barrier with my request. People began laughing, and the girls in my group looked at me as if I was crazy.

"Facebook, are you serious?" One of my friends mocked my bold attempt with a crooked smile.

"I know. I don't even know why I said it, but I did. Why am I like this?" I held my face with my hands in a slightly exaggerated state of despair.

"Well, at least he knows you're of age because you said Facebook and not TikTok," one of my friend's husbands pointed out.

I had aged myself somewhat, but it had been the only way I could think of to connect. It was easy, familiar, and accessible. Private mission number two was accomplished. If he was interested, Dale would get in contact, and if he wasn't, I could at least say that I gave it a shot.

The group immediately returned to the vibe our crew had

been enjoying the entire week. We ended the night on a high note, heading out to grab a bite to eat on Circuit Avenue. Circuit was a main artery where you could eat, bar hop, shop, and all that jazz. In the middle of our meal, I excused myself to the bathroom, and when I returned, a friend alerted me to look at my phone. I grabbed my phone and saw the group text thread with all my girlfriends. There were texts saying, "No way... Hell naw... You lying." I continued to scroll to the top, where one of my friends was trying to get my attention.

> Nora: "Coco, you're never going to believe it! Secret Service is looking for you. He's walking around Circuit Avenue right now, looking for you. He gave me his number... call that man!"

&#x2767;

I sat in disbelief. There was no way that this was all happening to me. It was like a cheesy scene in a rom-com, and I was the lead female character. Dale had randomly approached my girlfriend and a bunch of folks wearing alum gear and asked if they had been to the reception at Garde East, the restaurant. They recognized him immediately.

The next thing to come out of his mouth was "Where's Coco?" The group he approached included my friend, Nora, and her husband, Adrian. They chatted with him on Circuit Avenue while I enjoyed dinner with the other half of our crew.

After dinner, we all met up. Nora and Adrian told me exactly how it happened. They heard him ask several groups before he reached the one they were in. Adrian showed Dale my LinkedIn profile to show him how to find me on Facebook after he asked for me by name. Dale gave them his number to give me when they saw me again. My friends urged me to call him immediately because it was our last night there. I played it cool and sent him a text instead.

Dale had my number and could make the next move whenever he wanted. My friends let me off the hook since I had contacted him, and we went back to enjoying our last night together. A few of us were craving some late-night snacks, so we stopped at Flavors and ended the night there for some dancing. Inside, the exposed brick walls were painted white, and there were outdoor tables where we could enjoy our meal on a Victorian-style porch. We were there for the late-night gathering and the atmosphere. They were playing some good old-school R&B and hip-hop.

It was Black joy on the dance floor. I felt that ultimate feeling of euphoria, the tingles from a good song, with everyone hyped and enjoying the vibes. Everyone sang with passion, and we danced to some variation of the hustle—a nostalgia where you felt like you were living two moments simultaneously. The past and the present blended in a living deja vú. I remembered the cabbie's history storytelling and wondered if this club had been open and held the same Black joy as this decades ago. It felt like the best way to end the trip: dancing with my friends, laughing, and letting go of the weight of the world in a place that felt safe.

I twirled around, and there he was with his tall, bald, handsome caramel complexion. I could see he was scoping out any and every girl in the bar with braids, which I happened to be rocking for this vacation.

I shouted his name from across the bar, an echo of shouting across the busy room earlier that day. He heard me and approached me on the dance floor.

"Hey, I've been looking for you."

Before I could respond, he scooped me up and gave me the biggest bear hug ever. Startled, I smiled from ear to ear like a child on Christmas morning.

Dale was no longer wearing his professional attire, which had made him stoic and stiff. His whole demeanor was more relaxed, a vibe I enjoyed just as much as his business persona. He wore a light blue collared short-sleeved shirt and jeans. It made him look handsomely boyish and ready to have a good time. Even though the club was loud and the lights were dim, time seemed to stop for us to inhale the moment.

"I texted you," I said, wanting him to know that the interest was not one-sided. His apparent interest gave me a bit of a rush after being single for a few years.

He looked down at his phone and saw the text. "Oh, dammit. Sorry, I don't get good service here. How long you here for?"

"Only until tomorrow." I saw his face fall, and he made an exaggerated pout with his lips.

"What time?" he asked.

"Twelve-thirty," I replied.

"Can I take you out to breakfast?"

"Yeah." I liked that he got straight to the point and seemed intent on spending more time with me. It caught my interest.

"I work out around seven," he said. "We can meet at Linda Jean's at eight-thirty."

I had no idea where Linda Jean's was, and started to say, "I don't even know where—"

My friends jumped in, screaming, "She'll be there! We'll get her there!"

I laughed, a little embarrassed but also appreciating their support. I hadn't realized they were hovering to make sure the conversation went smoothly.

# PERSISTENCE

Thank God my hair was in braids. When I woke up, it was already scorching outside, and I was immediately soaked in sweat. The air was so humid that even the first seconds after a shower weren't refreshing. I couldn't remember what it felt like to be cool. After drying myself completely, I found sweat already dripping down my back and underneath my breasts, just putting on undergarments. I dressed in front of the fan, wishing that the house we rented had central AC rather than these weak window units and fans.

Monique knocked on my door to make sure I was awake and ready. I was definitely awake, but I wasn't sure I was ready. I didn't want to have a stench that repelled him on our first official time together.

"Coco, relax. Let's focus on what's in our control—which isn't the weather!" Monique said. "You look great."

We looked up directions. The restaurant he had chosen was on Circuit Avenue, not far from our house, but the humidity made the shortest walk feel like an all-day desert hike. According to our internet search, Linda Jean's has been a staple in Oak Bluffs for almost fifty years, so I figured I was in good hands as far as the service and food were concerned.

On my two-block walk to Linda Jean's, I kept my eye out for any little shops I might be able to duck into for a little AC reprieve, but they were all closed. I kept thinking, *He's going to be a no-show. I'm going through all this trouble for nothing.* I was drenched with sweat by the time I reached the entrance to the purple Victorian house where the restaurant was housed. Inside, the browns and beiges contrasted with the outside of the restaurant. The restaurant was packed. It had a quaint, old-school Cheers atmosphere where everybody knows everybody's names.

The air inside felt even thicker, like an unnecessary wool blanket covering me. I felt like I was choking down the air instead of breathing it. *What a way to make a first impression, with sweat stains everywhere.* I looked around and didn't see him.

When he walked up and greeted me with his tall beauty, my apprehension increased. I didn't look or feel as well put-together as he did. He escorted me to the bar counter with an air of confidence that felt like he was somehow a regular here. Before we sat down, he hugged me tightly. I felt like a freshly squeezed California orange, continuing to drip sweat from every body part.

"I promise you I'm not nervous, just really hot." I found myself explaining my drench while I was still caught up in his embrace. He didn't seem to be as affected as I was by the weather. *What an unfavorable first-date impression.* He let go of me, saw that I was not exaggerating, and handed me some napkins. I used them to dab sweat off myself, but bits of the napkin were left behind wherever they touched my skin—two for two on the embarrassed front. I decided to worry less and focus on showing up authentically.

The waitress anticipated his order of scrambled eggs with bacon and apple juice before he had a chance to tell her.

"I guess I've been here a few times recently." He laughed.

I asked for an omelet with spinach, tomatoes, and onions with a veggie bowl side. When I chose the veggie bowl and no toast, Dale said "Good." I downed three glasses of water to cool down.

We jumped right into chatting and getting to know one another.

I soon forgot about the sweaty introductions as our conversation flowed smoothly and naturally. Both of us spoke candidly about our divorces and families. We showed each other pictures of our children. I felt safe in his presence. He was quirky and made me laugh, though sometimes I did wonder what his deal was. Quickly, though, he felt like a good friend, someone I could get along with. It felt like we had plenty in common, and our differences meshed well. It was a casual but genuine first date, and I felt myself drawn to him.

After breakfast, we meandered our way back to the house where I was staying, but again, the time was too short. He wasn't quite ready to say goodbye, and I wasn't either. I had a flight to catch, and he needed to prepare for work. He bent to hug me. He was six-foot-five to my mere five-foot-six, so he towered above me.

"Coco, call or text me when you get to the airport, okay?"

"I will." I felt cared for and flattered that he wanted to check up on me and make sure I got to my flight safely.

ॐ

Settling into my window seat on the plane next to a friendly older woman, I pulled out my journal to jot down some thoughts about my week. I exhaled deeply. My trip to Martha's Vineyard had been precisely what I needed. I had felt free and removed from all the pressure and expectations of daily life. It felt like a surreal trip back to childhood in some ways. As the eldest of four children, my childhood had a certain mix of innocence, playing outside until the street lights came on, sneaking off to the Brewster projects, and parenting my younger brother and sisters while still trying to understand the world around me. The limitations of my family had kept my worldview narrow for many years. Martha's Vineyard felt like the positive aspects of my childhood before I saw the flaws—innocent, relaxing, and carefree.

When I got a bit older and had more life experiences, both of hardship and joy, I gained new perspectives on my childhood household and upbringing. I realized that, despite the innocence, there were also many aspects of my childhood environment that were unhealthy. My parents were the first committed relationship I was exposed to, with their many challenges, and then, my extended family members, who also struggled with relationships. My father's parents had complex relationships, with multiple partners as my grandfather sought a woman who could bear him a son. He ended up having over ten children with multiple women. He was a prominent figure in Liberian politics and was murdered during the civil war for political reasons. My father had to navigate complex cultural dynamics between the patriarchy of Liberia and then his experiences as an immigrant in America.

As a young child, the examples I had were all I knew to emulate. I expected and didn't yet know to notice and name the toxicity, and so I played with friends, went to school, and walked through the world, unaware that my foundation in relationships was tainted. I spent a lot of time and effort in therapy unpacking these deep-rooted beliefs, but I still questioned myself, so meeting Dale at Martha's Vineyard conjured a mixture of excitement and hesitancy in me.

I pulled out my phone and smiled as I wrote a text to Dale: "Flight was delayed, but I'm heading home finally!"

&#x2763;

In my therapy session that week, I shared the experience of meeting Dale with my therapist.

"Oh wow, you met someone!" Her eyebrows went up a little. "So how are you feeling about dating again?"

"I think I'm feeling... mostly open to meeting someone and getting out there."

"Feeling open... tell me more about Dale."

"Well, he's kind of quirky. It felt comfortable overall, but I'm not sure if I might be projecting my past issues. He mentioned some problems in past relationships."

"Mmm... He could have scars similar to yours and just not be in a place to handle it as well as you."

"Yeah, I guess so. I just want to be able to set boundaries that are healthy."

"That's a really good goal. I'm happy that you're in a place where you're feeling ready to set these healthy boundaries, and that you can communicate from a place not based in fear." She smiled, and I nodded. It felt good to be making progress, even though I had some reservations about putting myself out there again.

"I do have some fears though..." I said, trailing off. "I'm remembering Clyde, my ex."

"What's coming up for you about Clyde right now?"

"Well, we fought all the time. He gaslit me and manipulated me, so I used to just withdraw and try to keep the peace and avoid fights. We had patterns where he questioned everything I said, so I ended up afraid to say anything or speak my truth. He was always undermining me and breaking our plans, like when he shortened his trip on my birthday weekend without telling me."

"What happened then?"

"Well, I asked what changed and why the shortened trip, and he pivoted from a simple question to defensiveness, saying, 'You have no idea how much I had to do to make this happen. I have so much going on at work.' I told him I always try to be understanding but also need communication. If he needed to change the plans, he should just talk about it. Instead of understanding me, he responded with, 'I don't know if I'm coming anymore, I feel like the energy is off, and you're always accusing or antagonizing or looking for a fight.' With him, I always felt like he was pissing on my leg but telling me that it was raining outside."

She nodded. "He really made you doubt yourself, and you want to make sure things are different in this new possible relationship."

ᴄᴈ

Over the next six weeks, Dale seemed determined to create a meaningful bond between us. He communicated constantly and learned my schedule during the week. I woke up every morning at 6:20 a.m., so he would call me at 6:21 a.m. Occasionally, he slept in and called me at 7:30 a.m., remembering that I would have just put my kids on the bus. He remembered critical details about my life, which I took as a compliment and sign that he thought highly of me. It felt like he was really trying to get to know me, the things I liked, and how I moved throughout life. He was acutely aware of my surroundings from afar, which felt a little strange. I would be in my office or kitchen when he called, and based on the background echo, he would say, "Sounds like you're in the kitchen, am I right?" He was a Secret Service agent, so I figured his training had taught him to be highly alert and pay attention to these little details.

The more I learned about his personality, the more those qualities fit into his daily life. What had come off a bit weird initially became more familiar as we got to know each other.

I did recognize that he was emotionally immature in some ways, which made me wonder a few times about how invested I wanted to be with him. Maturity would be huge, especially in times of conflict. I needed my next partner to be able to handle difficult situations to ensure we came out on the other side of it stronger as a couple.

Sometimes, when Dale tried to be funny, it didn't come off as such. It could be a bit bothersome, but it seemed harmless. A few times, I thought about cutting off communication because I wasn't quite sure this was the right person to forge a relationship with. But the constant attention from a handsome man felt validating, and I didn't feel like there were clear enough red flags to make me end our communication.

We had many conversations about our family history. After learning that I was of Liberian descent, he dove into Liberia's history and used that to capture my attention. I was folding my kids' laundry one night after they were in bed and chatting with him on the phone.

"Okay, I bet you didn't know this," he started.

"What?" I asked.

"Okay, did you know that Liberia began in the early nineteenth century as a project of the American Colonization Society, based on the idea that Black people would face better chances for freedom and prosperity in Africa than in the United States?"

"Dale, are you reading off Wikipedia right now to me? Are you serious?" We both laughed.

He totally was. I was delighted—finding a prospective partner who displayed interest on so many levels was rare. In my childhood, being African wasn't cool, but now, it felt like everyone wanted to connect to the diaspora. It was a welcome sense of pride, but it still felt a little tentative, because the ten-year-old version of me deep down remembered the insecurity I felt when someone called me an "African booty scratcher."

One morning he asked me about my previous marriage. "Tell me about your ex."

"My ex... well, James and I met in 2009, and he proposed within a year. I wouldn't exactly say I settled—that sounds harsh—but I guess I was just looking for something really different from my parents' marriage. It felt safe and reliable. And it gave security."

"I get that. What do you think made it go downhill?"

"Well, I think I wanted a more profound connection. We had kids, and that took so much attention. Then after we got comfortable as parents, I realized that I loved him, but I wasn't really in love with him. We did therapy together, and individually, but it just felt like something was missing."

"I feel that. What was missing, do you think?"

I paused at his question, reflecting. "I don't know, maybe it was more that I'd changed. I wasn't the insecure Black girl in a mostly white suburb anymore, looking for the approval of others. I wasn't afraid the world might see me as an angry Black woman anymore. I was more ready to be assertive and change the status quo. And it turned out that my work ethic and assertiveness were really helpful in my career, too. So it was just time—it was like I grew out of the relationship."

"I totally feel that. It's the same with my ex-wife. I still care about her, but we just grew apart."

&#8531;

Contentment with our communication filled my days. As our conversations deepened, a spark ignited within me. This newfound possibility emerged from the ashes of one of the most toxic relationships of my adult life. My doubts lingered, though. I didn't want my past to prevent me from forging new relationships, but I didn't want to rush into anything. I faced a choice. Was I willing to open myself up to the potential of a deeper connection with him, or should I put the brakes on progress before it went further than I was ready for? The prospect of vulnerability with another man loomed large in my mind. I needed to feel sure I was ready to explore this new path with him, setting clear boundaries and holding firm to my expectations.

During our conversations, I found myself empathizing with him. I was drawn to him, and having a prospect felt good. I was chatting with another guy at the time, but that didn't feel like anything serious.

I found myself looking forward to calls with him. Dale told me about the death of his mother, the end of his marriage, his relationships with his siblings, and parenting his only child. He was a phenomenal storyteller who had me on the edge of my seat with his tales. We were building a solid friendship—maybe more—and I wasn't quite sure how it all would play out. We were learning about each other. Even with the geographical distance, I still felt like I was in good hands most of the time. He made me laugh, and I looked forward to the check-ins and storytelling.

Other times, some of his interaction patterns rubbed me the wrong way. He sent me a selfie of him while he was in Detroit, and I responded back that he looked handsome. He texted back to tell me that I was "kind of pretty." Kind of pretty—was that supposed to be a compliment? I felt like it would be more affirming for him to say he thought I was pretty, without qualifying it, but he was determined to give me a half-compliment. When I questioned it, he texted back:

"That's a Dale stage five compliment. You haven't made it to stage five yet."

CЗ

I felt a little uncomfortable. A little voice inside asked me if he was trying to undermine me somehow. I hesitated to deepen our connection because of these moments of immaturity in which he seemed to act more like a man-child than a mature adult. Reflecting on these moments, though, I told myself that we all have flaws and areas of improvement. After all, nobody's perfect, right?

Dale opened up to me about his upbringing, recounting instances when he and his twin brother would steal bread to eat in their room, a memory that seemed to evoke a confusing mix of emotions in him. Sometimes, sharing these personal experiences seemed to make him pause. I would pry to get to know him more and to help him open up and be vulnerable. I could feel his discomfort and sadness creep in when sharing stories of his past, and then he would shut down and try to change the subject. He'd often say things like "Ugh, you're making me soft..." His voice would shift, or his eyes would reveal that he was holding back or afraid to be vulnerable.

Other times, however, he spoke more freely, reflecting a more profound complexity to his past. He often spoke about frequent arguments with his ex-wife, a topic that struck a chord with me because they resonated with my own childhood family dynamics and my parents' conflicts. On FaceTime one night, he said, "This one time, my ex and I were driving from Chicago back to Detroit. The constant bickering was just too much."

"I can understand that," I said, wiping down the kitchen counters while I listened to his story.

He continued, "I couldn't picture it ever getting better. And I remember we were driving over a bridge and I just thought about driving off because I didn't want to keep living like this."

I kept my face still, trying not to react. I had a flash in my mind to my kindergarten teacher, who also taught my favorite dance class.

"You know," I said, "this story reminds me of my favorite teacher. She lived down the street from us, and I looked up to her like an aunt. She was gentle, kind of eccentric... the neighborhood kids and I loved to go dance at her house even though she and her husband fought often. One day, though, when I went to her backdoor, I found crowds of police swarming inside and outside.

Her husband had killed her and then killed himself."

He stared at me through the screen. He looked shocked. Maybe he didn't know what to say. I didn't either.

One morning he told me nonchalantly, "This one time when I was a kid, I was playing outside with a friend, and there was this stupid stray cat who kept trying to grab our toy. We got annoyed with the cat, and so I went and got some rope and a bat. We tied the cat to a fence and struck it with the bat until it went quiet."

My ears were ringing, and I couldn't believe what I was hearing. *Did he just admit to torturing a helpless animal?* "What? Dale, did you untie the cat? Did you check on the cat after? Did you see the cat in the neighborhood again?"

He didn't remember. We moved on and talked about other things, but I was bothered by this story.

These interactions left me feeling emotional whiplash, but the demands of work, travel, and parenting kept me from dwelling on them too much. My uncertainty was overshadowed by the more pressing demands in my life. At one point, I stopped responding to him altogether. There was too much living to be done to continue to deal with his childishness. I had three children of my own and didn't need another one in my life.

He kept calling and texting though. He kind of Urkeled me, wearing me down with persistence. It felt harmless, and I second-guessed whether he was trying to get to know me for romantic purposes. Either way, I enjoyed having someone to talk to daily.

As we communicated more, I began to feel like there might be some compatibility. I learned about his likes and dislikes. There were more positives than negatives to our budding friendship. He expressed his brokenness, emphasizing his need to connect, and I, too, desired a connection. I saw no harm in letting things play out and seeing where they went. Our conversations delved deeper, exciting me at the potential for a beautiful relationship to blossom.

I discussed our conversations with my therapist, who gave me advice on how to handle things and create a safe space for communication. Despite his intermittent immaturity, Dale started to feel like he could fit into my world. I was someone who was drawn to help others, and he seemed like a project that, if handled with care, could be the missing link to my love life.

Waiting to pick my son up one afternoon, I sat with my thoughts for a few minutes. I sensed a profound loneliness in Dale, mirroring my own yearning for love and connection. I had never really experienced a truly genuine connection in my past relationships, which was a factor in why I continued to engage with Dale. We connected over our shared experiences with parental relationships, the absence of "I love yous" in our upbringing, and insecurities.

We'd both been the awkward Black kid in school. He was shy and unsure of himself growing up, and as outgoing as I was, I was the quintessential Black girl from Detroit. I remembered something he'd said recently— "You're intriguing. You have beauty, humor, intelligence, sexiness, and a touch of hood and tomboy all rolled up into one. Not something a brother comes across that often." With Dale, I didn't feel the need to conceal any part of myself; I could be authentic, and I encouraged him to do the same.

Taking care of others had always been important to me, and I could sense Dale's sadness and tendency to lean on me for support. I responded to his needs—I had lacked support in my childhood and often felt I could give it to someone else to heal my own lack. Our conversations were filled with excitement, especially when I laughed at his stories and encouraged him to share more. I felt like the highlight of his day.

One evening, we discovered that we would both be in Napa Valley at the same time in October. He asked if I could extend my trip by a few days so we could meet and spend time together. Why not? We made all the arrangements. It seemed like an opportunity to figure out how I felt about this new person who seemed to want to be a part of my life. *Was it worth my time to continue to get to know him better? Was it just a friendship, or did he want there to be more between us?* It was time for me to take stock of this man and decide what I wanted from him, if anything.

The push and pull I felt toward him from day to day, sometimes minute to minute, was so confusing. *The only way I could be sure,* I thought, *was to meet him in Napa.* Then I could make a more confident decision on what I desired. We would have time to talk face-to-face, and I hoped it would bring me the clarity I needed to get off the roller coaster of maybe, maybe not.

# CARMEL BY THE SEA

It felt like I blinked and October was here. I packed and prepared to attend an old friend's wedding in Napa Valley. The Obamas were scheduled to be in Napa Valley at the same time.

"So, you're actually interested in a romantic relationship? This isn't a friend zone thing?" I prodded when he offered to let me stay in his room to save money.

"I feel like I've been laying the foundation for more than friendship," he admitted.

I contemplated his approach, style of conversation, and intentions, concluding that this was simply his way of doing things. While it didn't align with my methods, I couldn't fault him for being authentic. Like any potential couple, we had areas we needed to work on. I didn't want to dismiss him for being different, nor did I want to be disregarded for my own idiosyncrasies. I hoped we would both remain open, be willing to compromise when necessary, and continue building our connection through meaningful conversations.

He began to plan our time together immediately after I decided to extend my visit. I found this attractive. He was intentional about asking about my likes and dislikes and things I appreciated while on vacation. His attention to my preferences allowed me to let down more of my walls. I told him my favorite foods and the restaurants I frequented. He learned about my love for French rosé, specifically those from the Provence region. Dale was proactive about the trip, which made me see him in a positive light.

At the last minute, the Obamas changed their plans and went to Carmel by the Sea instead of Napa Valley. Dale called me, panicking. While we were talking on the phone, he was on Kayak looking for flights from Napa Valley to Carmel. While he went back and forth with flights and options for me, my spirit settled in a cool, collected space––he was proactive with problem-solving, and unlike Clyde, he wasn't blaming me for last-minute changes to our plans. As reassuring as it was that he was committed to making our visit happen and looking for solutions to the problem, I also thought paying over a thousand dollars to transport me thirty minutes to his location was ludicrous. I wasn't sure if I was comfortable with him spending that much, especially since I hadn't completely settled on whether we were heading toward a serious relationship. It felt like the trip would be the deciding factor, although I had contemplated it plenty over the last six weeks.

"Dale, I can figure out a way to get there without you paying a thousand dollars for a thirty-minute flight," I said.

My friend's wedding events were underway, and Dale was persistent in asking about what I had packed to wear. It seemed pretty normal for a heterosexual man. In my experience, they tend to be into thighs, breasts, and hourglass figures. Dale was a butt man, but he had made multiple comments about how, when we first met, he hadn't checked mine out. I dismissed the comments and told him how weird he was being. When we had had breakfast back at Martha's Vineyard, he remarked, "You know, I find you attractive and funny, but I've never checked out your ass." What a strange thing to say!

When I asked him what he meant, he said it was because I was significantly shorter than he was and claimed that I was not of average height. He even looked up the average height of American women, which is five foot four, and I'm five foot six, but he continued to call me shorty. He kept searching through my Instagram and Facebook pics to see if he could get an angle on my butt, then would take screenshots of specific images and comment, "Oh, I see... You got a little something going on back there." I didn't really like how he handled sensitive topics such as my figure or how he felt about me.

We talked about what I would wear to the wedding, but the romper I wanted to wear no longer fit well. I didn't want my ass hanging out the back of the jumpsuit. He asked me to send him a picture, which I did. He found it amusing, but his teasing about my height and figure didn't feel complimentary. He added emojis, double-stating things, maybe for effect, but I just found it... interesting. The fixation gave me pause. If he aimed to develop a deeper relationship, I needed him to adjust how he complimented me—more direct and less teasing.

Not only did Dale tease me about my height and backside, he commented on my bridesmaid dress, saying that I looked more like I was going out somewhere to "drop it like it's hot," meaning that I looked more like I was heading to the club than dressing for a wedding. He praised my cousin's dress, but I was left without a compliment. It felt like he was throwing me shade left and right. I began second-guessing going to Carmel.

I attended the wedding with my cousin, who rented a car, and she offered to drive the ninety minutes down to Carmel. Obviously, we talked about Dale. I caught her up on what everyone else in my life was privy to—that Dale could possibly be a new love interest. My goal for the trip was to spend more time with him so I could decide whether he was a contender. On the drive, my cousin and I chatted about how Dale and I had met at Martha's Vineyard and how we've been communicating daily since our initial meet and first date.

As we got closer to Carmel, I could feel my nerves on edge. I wanted to address the distasteful comments he made about my dress for the wedding, but I felt apprehensive, knowing the timing had to be right—I had no plans to greet him and dive into some big heart-to-heart. The outcome of this conversation felt like it would dictate whether I stayed or returned home.

My cousin and I went back and forth on the drive down about my decision not to let Dale pay for the flight.

"Coco, you were just trying to avoid being inconvenient. You should've let him show you that he cares! It's his money and he's a grown man who can make his own decisions."

"Yeah, but a *thousand* dollars for a half-hour flight? We don't even know what we are yet... We could have so much fun with a thousand dollars, too."

We ended up with us agreeing to disagree. Anyway, we were already most of the way there, so it was a silly debate to keep having.

As we drove, towering redwoods lined our path, creating a majestic canopy overhead. The road to Carmel was a scenic marvel, winding gracefully along the picturesque coastline. My research had vividly portrayed this place, highlighting its renowned attractions: the pristine white sand beaches, the enchanting European-style village, and the inviting turquoise waters that beckoned to be explored.

I was trying not to make a pros and cons list of having a relationship with Dale like some middle schooler, but also I wanted to be intentional about having a clear mind and being more vocal to address the hurtful comments instead of just letting them go, like I had in previous relationships. My cousin and I both were back in the dating game after divorce, so we were mulling over what was out there and how to communicate and advocate for ourselves, while also being open and not just cutting people off at the first sign of shortcomings. My cousin finally said, "Just enjoy yourself!"

❧

Dale was waiting outside to meet me and help me with my bags. He greeted me with a big bear hug, and my frustrations relaxed. I was prepared to discuss my feelings with him calmly. Face-to-face, I knew we could talk and resolve it like adults. We took the elevator, and he gave me a quick tour of the property as we headed to the room. I could feel myself settling into my authentic self and feeling more confident about our encounter.

When we entered our hotel room, I noticed that he had stocked the room with water and my favorite snacks: kale chips, seaweed, and cashews, along with some rosé. He listened attentively when I spoke, and his attention to detail made me feel seen. In times like these, he could melt my heart and bring me back to the center again.

He alerted me about the dinner reservations he had made for us. I found his proactive nature so endearing. Dale was willing to change and work on behaviors that could harm our relationship, which distinguished him from my ex. It made me feel optimistic about having a future with him and more willing to accept some of his weaknesses.

I unpacked so that I could get ready for dinner. Earlier, during our conversations about preparing for the trip to Carmel, we had discussed our attire. Dale had shared suit options to coordinate with what I was wearing. He also sent me menus from multiple restaurants to choose from. Upon arrival, I wanted to take a quick shower after being in the car all day. I freshened up quickly so we could head out to the dinner reservation. I knew that we weren't "just friends," but I also wanted to be respectful, and so far we'd only hugged... so I came out of the bathroom with my towel on and went straight to my dress to put it on without revealing too much. Dale stood with two suits in hand to see which one I preferred. I chose his tuxedo pants and jacket with no tie to complement the earth tones of my dress.

He noticed that I was struggling to reach behind my own back and zip up my dress. "Want a hand?"

"Sure," I said.

He gently moved my hair aside to slowly zip up my dress, making sure not to pull too hard or tug. I could feel the butterfly tingles and goosebumps in a wave across my body. I was also aware suddenly that I found him extremely handsome, and our chemistry was not subtle. Before heading out to the Uber, I glanced at his side of the bed and noticed his large cowboy boots. Seeing a tall Black man from the hood with cowboy boots was unique. I smiled and appreciated his quirky personality.

The restaurant complimented our mood and provided an atmosphere of romance and beauty. The host directed us to a table on the patio. On his arm, I felt womanly, protected, and safe—a feeling that I had lacked in my previous serious relationship. Always the gentleman, he pulled out my chair, and I had a seat. It was Thursday, and we both blurted out how we were missing Thursday Night Football. I pulled out my phone so we could watch the game in the background.

When our waitress arrived, I ordered a glass of French rosé. "I always know the difference between French rosés and other ones," I told Dale.

He was skeptical and ordered another kind, challenging me to tell the difference. Of course, I passed the taste test and proved his doubts wrong.

"Okay then," he conceded. We smiled at each other.

Shortly after, I brought up the interaction about the wedding dress. I told him I had considered not coming to Carmel because of his attitude. He was shocked to learn I had considered not coming and thanked me for giving him the chance to make amends. He admitted that I didn't know him well enough to understand his personality and his attempts at humor. He acknowledged that his playful banter was hurtful and said he hadn't meant it.

He grabbed my hand across the table and said, "I think you're absolutely gorgeous, your dress was gorgeous, and I should've told you that immediately. I'm glad you didn't cancel coming to see me."

His response seemed thoughtful, and I didn't feel dismissed, so I let the incident go and forgave him.

Dale asked about a tattoo on my arm.

"Oh, I was in a relationship that was toxic. This open heart tattoo is a symbol of what I've been through. There was a lot of gaslighting, and it hurt me. Therapy has helped me heal and grow from the experience. Now it's a reminder to keep my heart open."

Dale was empathetic to my history, and I felt comfortable sharing myself with him because I didn't feel judged. We sat silently for several long seconds before he broke the silence.

"I admire you so much. You've been through a lot, but you're still optimistic."

He seemed more relaxed and accommodating in person than over the phone. I was at ease, which made the process of reconciling quicker and smoother, allowing me to return to feeling connected with him. His jokes were funny, and the man's ability to lighten a mood without being immature was a great fresh start to the rest of our evening together.

The atmosphere was comfortable, playful, innocent, and invigorating. I loved how we bounced off each other and never had a dull moment. Whenever I mentioned any concerns, he was always receptive, so it was hard to stay in a mood when I felt validated and heard.

We dove deeper into each other's past relationships. He talked about how much he and his ex had argued, and we discussed how my seemingly great relationship had turned sour. Dale told me about a relationship he had after his divorce and how he knew he wasn't in love. He said, "We just weren't in the same place in life, so why hold her back?" In these moments, I felt comfortable as I observed his vulnerability.

As the evening wore on, we found ourselves downtown Carmel at a karaoke bar. He was enthusiastic to participate, exclaiming and hollering like it was a sports event for a team he cared about. I didn't love karaoke, but his excitement was contagious as he shared his passion for singing karaoke when he traveled. His face lit up, and like a kid, before signing up for his song, he dug his long arms into the candy jar. He passed over the Snickers, Skittles, and Twix, and landed on a Tootsie Pop. He smoothly took my hand and led me close to the stage. Finally, his name was called. He sang "My Own Worst Enemy" by Lit.

It was close to midnight when he finished his lively rendition. I clapped, but I could feel myself fading and starting to get tired. His nerdiness had unlocked my heart, though. I wasn't feeling as conflicted anymore.

The following morning, he nudged me awake and asked if I wanted to join him at the hotel gym for his typical morning workout. He had the same routine every day. When we were at home, he'd wake up and call me as he was heading to the gym first thing in the morning, no matter where he was.

"No, thanks. This bed is too comfy. You have a good workout," I said, and rolled over to go back to sleep.

He woke me up again when he returned, and I lay in bed, feeling lazy, while he showered. We ate a hearty omelet breakfast together at the hotel and shared stories about our careers. After breakfast, we walked the property and played darts and backgammon.

I had gone from feeling unsure about the trip to not wanting him to leave without me. I was sitting on the bed while he put on his clothes for work when he gently grabbed my face and pulled me in for a kiss. It was the first time we had kissed, and it felt natural within the flow of the morning. His lips were soft.

He texted me during his shift, checking on me to see what I was up to and ensuring I was safe and still enjoying myself.

That night, we watched the Jeffrey Dahmer Netflix series on my laptop and stayed up late talking. At some point, we fell asleep and enjoyed spooning time. I love spooning! He woke up around three in the morning and began talking again. By then, I just wanted to sleep, but I tried not to complain because he was talking about how comfortable I made him feel. I felt validated that I could provide the comfort he needed to express himself. I did want him to shut up though.

"Dale... isn't it time to sleep? Aren't you tired yet?"

He laughed and started trying to find a ticklish spot on my neck. He playfully ventured around the nape with a gentle caress from his nose and mouth. His warm breath was inviting, making me a little wet between my legs.

Then he quickly made his way down my body and put his face between my legs, face first. The move came out of nowhere. I felt amazed and shocked, all in the same breath. My mind was racing. *Thank goodness I was waxed.* I squeezed my legs to semi-smother him when he moved into my erogenous zones. *What the fuck, how did we get here?* I grabbed his ears to enjoy the ride but couldn't quite bring myself to be fully present and climax. My mind and body were in two different places.

Starting to get anxious, I faked an orgasm, moaning and grabbing at his neck. He rested his head on my chest, looked me straight in the eyes, and asked, "Did you cum?"

"Yes," I lied, trying to sound confident.

He grabbed me tightly and went to sleep within a few minutes.

ℭ

In the morning, as I packed up to leave for the airport, he watched me.

"Coco, I'll be on Oahu in three weeks for work. You ever been to Hawaii?"

"I haven't! Are you inviting me?" I was eager to see him again, and since I had never been to Hawaii, I knew it would be memorable. So we made a plan to see each other again in three weeks.

# TO THE ISLANDS

Dale changed his communication patterns with me after our discussion in Carmel, which I appreciated. He softened up and was much more direct with his intentions and words, though he was still quirky and goofy. I got the sense that there were layers to his personality he was afraid to share.

In his softer moments, Dale's vulnerability helped us connect on deeper levels and made me feel secure with the relationship. His willingness to share this side of him made him feel like a great choice to trust and engage with as a partner. So far, he showed positive growth. When he traveled, we talked frequently as he went from the airport to the terminal, before boarding, after landing, etc. He would FaceTime me every morning, and with the seven-hour difference between Central and Hawaiian time zones, this involved a significant effort on his part that made me feel special.

We were both excited to spend more time together in person. He was also eager to show me the sights since it was my first time visiting Hawaii. He wanted to show me all the regular spots he frequented. There was a UFC gym where he would often see The

Rock while he worked out. He frequented Workplay, a cigar bar with a jungle theme, though he didn't smoke. We discussed him taking me to Duke's on Waikiki, a restaurant on Waikiki beach that was named after a legendary surfer. He described it as kind of a tourist spot, decorated with stereotypical Hawaiian decor. He told me it was usually loud and packed with tourists, but the location was top-notch, with sunsets over the water that looked like they were out of a magazine. As we planned together, we balanced his go-to spots with what I love to do while on vacation, like beach walking, sunrises, sunsets, and new adventures. He said he didn't usually do things like that, but I wanted to get him out of his comfort zone.

I had anticipated taking photos of my arrival for Instagram. I disembarked the plane, eagerly looking through the crowd of people waiting. Dale wasn't there. I watched the Luau Girls put beautiful leis of orchids and deep red plumerias on my fellow passengers as they greeted their loved ones joyfully. Dale arrived at the airport fifteen minutes late and didn't have a lei for me, which disappointed me. He just laughed and picked me up for a big bear hug and a kiss. It didn't quite make up for not receiving a lei, but it was still warm and inviting.

We were staying at the Ala Moana Hotel in Honolulu. Their beautifully vaulted ceilings and colors that fell into the woods and waters made the atmosphere perfect. The main level had vaulted ceilings and white walls, with glass doors and walls that allowed natural light in. I could smell the salty sea air and feel the humidity inside the lobby due to the continuous opening of the main doors. There was a line of airline employees coming and going through the lobby. A long line of anxious folks waited for the one elevator to take them to the thirty-sixth floor for the famous Ala Moana happy hour.

I could feel excitement exuding from Dale as he showed me around and talked about our future plans. I felt like I could say or do anything with him, and he would go with the flow, as did I. After the tour, we went directly to our room. The room was okay, but definitely not five stars. When I commented that it was kind of basic, he laughed and reminded me that this was government money. I told myself that we'd be spending little time in the room—

only to sleep, shower, nap, and change.

He began to test the waters to find out what I was interested in doing. "Are you tired or hungry? Do you feel like doing anything?"

It was early evening, and I felt like a shower after the eight-hour flight. We decided we'd go up to the Signature Room once I felt refreshed and was ready to go. The Signature Room was a steakhouse on the thirty-sixth floor adorned in beige and deep reds, and accented by picture windows that give views of both the city and the ocean. It was beautiful and quite romantic. It felt like an ideal way to begin our time together—with a good meal and conversation.

Alex and Josh were his favorite bartenders at the Signature Room. They quickly became mine as well. Both of them were personable and likable. Josh was Hawaiian, well-mannered with a beautiful smile, and funny. He was attentive, just like you'd want a five-star bartender to be. Alex was a flirt! He was tall and handsome, with long hair like a Black Jesus. He used to play Division I football, and he had no filter! He was from the South and could code-switch between Hawaiian and Southern accents on cue. They were both so good at their jobs and keeping customers happy, the perfect duo behind the bar. Whenever Alex was distracted flirting or talking too much, Josh was right there picking up his slack. I developed good rapport with these two almost immediately. They kept track of my favorite drink, which was Tito's and Fever Tree ginger beer since they didn't serve a French rosé.

Dale and I had a lovely time at dinner. I ordered salmon, and Dale ordered his usual steak. I noticed that Dale ate more like a frat boy than a grown man. I thought his diet needed more vegetables and convinced him to add some sautéed spinach, asparagus, and broccoli to his meat and mashed potato dish. I loved their strawberry and arugula salad. The food was delicious, and the service was even better. The bartenders shared some of their favorite stories of Dale over dinner. I learned more about him, and during dinner, I soaked him in; every touch, smile, and even his smell had me on a high that overrode my exhaustion. We used our time to completely drown in each other's presence.

When we returned to the room, I noticed he had thoughtfully arranged water and my favorite snacks, ensuring all my needs were met. I appreciated his attentiveness and care. As we talked and cuddled that night, I began to feel closer to him, sensing the potential for love if this continued. Our conversation was engaging and intimate, fostering a sense of trust. However, for the second time, he surprised me by going down on me abruptly. We were lying in bed talking, and he jumped over from his side of the bed like an excited kid and lifted the blankets, opened my legs, lifted up my teddy, and went down. While it felt incredible, it also caught me off guard. Despite the initial surprise, I found myself immersed in the moment, enjoying the intimacy we shared.

Afterward, I broke the silence between us. "I'm going to be direct here."

"Okay," he said hesitantly, resetting himself next to me.

"Why do you keep doing that?" I asked.

"What are you talking about? Did you not like it?"

"I do, but why do you just keep doing that?" I paused, unsure how to word it. "I want the whole shebang! I want the appetizer, the meal, dessert, and then I want a cocktail at the end—not just the appetizer by itself." It was so startling the way he would hit me with pleasure out of nowhere; as suddenly as it began, it also abruptly went cold. We both laughed at the situation, so the mood remained light.

"Well, I wasn't really prepared the first time, and we had never spoken about it, so I wasn't sure."

"Yeah, we hadn't talked about it."

"I didn't have a condom, and I just really wanted to do that for you. But it would help to know what you like."

"Okay, so we could talk more... you could ask me questions about whether I like it sensual and soft, or rough, with music on or off, with lights on or off... if I like to be flipped, slapped, hair tugging, choked..." My directness opened the conversation up, and we began discussing our sexual preferences. I was happy to feel like he was interested in pleasing me and not just being pleased. For someone who spoke about being a selfish person, he did many selfless things for me. It felt like he was working on his weak spots, as I have done and continue to do. I had never experienced having such an in-depth conversation about my desire for intimacy.

The talk elevated our lovemaking—in creativity, frequency, and intensity. He learned that I was a bit of a risk-taker and enjoyed spontaneity, novel locations, and high frequency. I was sexually submissive and wanted him to know that he could take the lead.

One night, we were sitting outside on the patio deck talking about our past and having a glass of wine when he got out of his chair, dropped down to his knees, opened my legs, and shoved his head in between them. It went from zero to a hundred immediately, and we found ourselves having the most passionate sex on the patio. The risk of being seen or heard intensified the experience. Not only were we able to have deep conversations, share our lives, and enjoy each other's company in simple ways, but sex became an excellent bonus. It made me feel hopeful about our future, and I began to think he could be a lasting person in my life. He would do things out of his comfort zone to please me, and I was melting fast.

Dale was working the midday shift, which meant we had some time in the morning and late at night to spend with each other. One morning, I suggested we lie by the pool and hang out before he went to work. I wanted to get breakfast and take it slow that morning— sunbathe or hang out in the cabana and just revel in the natural beauty of Waikiki. It wasn't really his cup of tea, but he came with me. He hadn't packed swim trunks or flip-flops. I found it hilarious that he only had a pair of Timbs, gym shoes, and his work shoes.

When we were planning the activities for our trip, it came up that he had a skin condition called tinea versicolor, a fungal skin disease of the skin that causes small, discolored patches. His patches were mostly on his head and shoulders, so he often wore a baseball cap. Lots of the activities I wanted to do were outdoors, and he had to be careful not to spend too much time in direct sunlight. He shared that he'd had it since he was a child, and his mom took him to many doctors to figure out what was going on. I looked up his condition and found some good sunscreens for him to wear while we lay out by the pool.

We spent the morning precisely as I had wanted. I wore my brown one-piece swimsuit, and we headed down to the pool. He was so soft and sensual with me while we sat in the cabana. He knew it was important for me to be outside, so he picked a cabana that had both sun for me and shade for him. He brought down some rosé and snacks for us to enjoy, and as we lay there, he grabbed me and pulled me closer to rest with him. He began rubbing my thigh and massaging my hand with soft strokes. It was probably one of the first times I'd heard him sigh, and I asked him about it. He replied, "I understand why you like to relax and nap by water."

To accommodate him, I put a towel over the cabana to shade us more from direct sunlight. We listened to music while we just lay there for about two hours. I introduced him to Snoh Aalegra, and he enjoyed a few of the songs I played. We listened to the whole album, and my favorites became his: "I Want You Around," and "Do for Love." Those moments felt like heaven. Relaxing outdoors with someone you're newly connecting with on multiple levels brings clarity, a calm that I hadn't felt in a long time.

The day was heating up, and we were both pretty sweaty, so we went to take a dip in the pool. When I realized that it didn't have a shallow end, I just sat on the edge and swished my feet around to cool off.

"One time," he launched into a story, "I taught myself to swim by jumping into the deep end of a pool and damn near drowning. I wanted to jump off the diving board with all the other kids. I didn't know how to swim, but I observed the mechanics of it and decided to just try it. I did figure it out!"

I laughed, picturing the scene.

"And then one time during boot camp, I was going so fast that I ran out of steam and had to hurry over to the side to catch my breath."

Sometimes I felt like he approached our relationship similarly. He had just jumped in and tried to figure it out. Some days, he did well, while other times, he struggled. If he could conquer the swimming, I figured he might have the stamina with me as well.

He made sure that while he was swimming, he still gave me

attention as I sat on the side. I thought it was romantic and showed that he wasn't selfish. After a few laps around, he would come in between my legs and gently pour water down my thighs, caressing them as I sprinkled water on his head. He even offered for me to hang onto him so I could get further in the water without getting my hair wet, but I declined. He looked at me after motioning me to join him for a swim and I said no. He tapped his head and whispered, "Is it your hair, huh?"

I said, "Yep." I didn't want to get in the water because it was cold, and I also didn't want to ruin my hair.

The time seemed to fly by, and soon he announced that he had to prepare for work, so we headed back up to the hotel room.

☙

While taking a shower, he noticed some of my toiletries, and he was so inquisitive that he looked up the products to learn more about them. He walked out of the hotel bathroom with my loofah, body butter, and Honey Pot in his hands.

"Made by humans with vaginas for humans with vaginas... Is that why you taste so good?"

Dale could make me blush and smile simultaneously, and I was getting a little sad that he would be leaving soon. I knew he was coming back, but I just wanted to hog every second with him. It was easy to be with him.

He asked about the benefits of my loofah and asked if he could use it. I said yes since it was his first time—he had to pop a few of his cherries somehow. He was excited about the experience and how his skin felt afterward. I purchased him his own loofah because he loved it so much. Sharing a loofah was like sharing a toothbrush for me—a big no. As he was getting ready, the man asked to use my body butter; he had his own lotion but used mine all up. His big ass needed his own, but he did end up replacing it.

Dale took an interest in everything about me. Like when I was getting my nails done for the trip to Hawaii, I sent him a picture of my nails; he noticed the coordinates tattoo on my wrist and looked

39

them up to find the correct location. Later, he questioned me about its location and why I had it tattooed on my wrist. In true Dale fashion, he joked that it was either my prison yard number, answers to a high school math test, or coordinates to a hidden treasure.

I played the afternoon by ear, letting my spirits lead me. He continued to text me all day while he was at work. He apologized for being gone for so long and told me that he would try to get off early. I didn't want him to worry about it. I had known that he would be working and didn't want him doing anything that could jeopardize his employment.

I spent some time with the bartenders in the Signature Room and grabbed dinner there. There were plenty of guests solo traveling, coming in and out. I had the opportunity to meet people from all over. The hotel hosted a lot of government employees and people from the airlines. Dale wasn't off until nine that night, so I headed back to the room to chill for a while before getting ready. When he returned from work, we planned to head to Workplay.

He wanted me to experience hip-hop night at Workplay. I wanted to make sure I looked and felt my best. As I was doing my makeup, Dale walked through the hotel room door. Even though I had told him that it wasn't necessary, he had asked to get off work early so that we could hang out. I thought it was a sweet gesture that made me feel important to him. I felt like being with me mattered to him, and I didn't have to beg for his attention; he was as interested in me as I was in him.

After enjoying some music at Workplay, we drove to Waikiki Beach for a late-night walk on the beach. I took off my sandals because the tide was coming in. Dale walked on the beach with Timberland boots on. I laughed, shook my head at the sight, and told him to take off his boots.

"Roll up your pants so that the bottom doesn't get wet and sandy," I said.

It was a beautiful scene: us walking hand-in-hand, surrounded by the sounds of the waves. We walked over a mile, our toes in the sand and water as the tide came in. The water was the perfect temperature, and Waikiki strip was lit up so beautifully against the shoreline.

"Do you want a picture?" he asked.

"No, I want to just remember this from memory," I said.

As we drove back to the hotel from a wonderful night out, he said, "Driving with you is so peaceful."

It was such a specific compliment, and it felt like there was a story there somewhere, so I asked, "What?"

"You don't say anything or criticize."

"Why would I criticize you? I'm a passenger princess."

"Well, when I would drive in the car with my ex, it wasn't peaceful. She criticized me all the time. I had gotten used to that, and with you, it's different."

His body language was relaxed, as if he'd just finished getting a massage, and his voice was similar to that feeling when you come home from a stressful day of work and hit the couch after pouring a glass of wine.

"What would she say or do?"

"From something as simple as parking spaces to screaming and arguing about something I didn't do exactly how she wanted me to. Anything and everything, really."

"Huh, okay. That just sounds like someone who doesn't like you."

The next day, we had breakfast, and he showed me around some more of his stomping grounds. I felt like I was on a field trip. While we were out and about, he asked, "Do you want to go to the Obamas'?"

I told him no, but he didn't take no for an answer.

"They're not there." He tried to cajole me, but I really wasn't interested.

"They aren't extending an invite to me, so I'm not going there uninvited. It feels weird and disrespectful to even consider." He had already sent me several photos of their house the week before, and although it was beautiful, I wasn't here for the Obamas—I was here for him.

"You already showed me pictures. I'm good."

As he kept pushing, I realized how important it was to him. It was a moment of pride for him, and it seemed like he was showing me a lot of his insecurities. I suggested I could get in trouble or get arrested, and he assured me that I wouldn't get arrested for being there because he was letting me in.

"Are you sure you don't want to come? Just come keep me company."

"Can't I get arrested for trespassing? I don't want to get you fired."

"No, you can't get in trouble from me giving you access. Anyway, I'm by myself today, so no one will know. If anything, I'm the one who could get in trouble."

Dale seemed to think that telling me that would appease me, but it felt like an even clearer indication that we shouldn't be there.

Against my better judgment, though, he convinced me to keep him company while he worked. He said we would just watch football.

The drive there was beautiful. I couldn't stop commenting on the coastline, the beaches and blue waters, the waves crashing, the surfers trying to catch a wave, and the mountain backdrop—all nature's perfection.

As he showed me around the Obamas' house, I could sense his pride in his career. He smiled ear to ear while giving me a tour. He speculated about the cost of everything and mentioned other celebrities who had visited the Hawaii property. Once we got outside, he brought me to this rock where he told me Barack often stood in the morning to view the beach and take in some deep breaths. He encouraged me to stand on the rock. It felt a bit strange for me, and I declined at first, but he kept insisting, "Stand on the rock! Who can say that they've done that?" in a very poor imitation of Barack Obama's voice. I stood on the rock.

I felt uncomfortable with how Dale's self-esteem seemed to be dependent on his profession and with how hard he was trying to impress me. Walking around their home, I wasn't proud of my decision to come, but Dale was beaming and excited to show me everything. I accepted the tour to celebrate him and his accomplishments because it was important to him, but I knew it was wrong to be there, and I felt like an intruder.

When we arrived back at the command center, he saw someone at the gate.

"Coco, let me just put you somewhere real quick."

My heart skipped a beat.

He led me to a dark server room. "I'll be right back."

I felt like I was in high school, ditching class or something. My mind was going a hundred miles an hour, thinking about all the bad ways this day could end. *Why did I let him convince me to come?*

He came back and whispered, "Follow me, come wait over here." He led me to the agent's bathroom, and I sat on the toilet until he came back.

Once things were calm, Dale came back to find me again, and we headed back to the command center to watch football. He kept showing me around and began to flirt like a teenager.

"We should have sex in Michelle's bathroom, like a mile-high club."

I couldn't believe he would suggest it. I felt so uncomfortable and all I wanted to do was go back to the hotel.

He sat next to me in a chair like a kid begging for candy, with pleading eyes, rubbing my leg. "Remember our conversation from last night about sexual desires? You said you wanted novelty and assertiveness," he blurted. "No one will ever be able to top this! Who can ever say they've had sex in Michelle Obama's bathroom? Even if you tell them, they won't believe us—but we'll know!"

My jaw dropped. On one hand, he was right, but on the other hand, I still felt uncomfortable being here without permission. I said, "No... I want to go back."

He had to stay, so he ordered an Uber to take me to the hotel. When the Uber arrived, the driver asked for Richard. I froze and looked at him in confusion. I didn't ask any questions, though, because I was ready to get out of there. I confirmed that the Uber driver had the correct address and got in.

Dale seemed to notice that I was uncomfortable and called me on the phone as the Uber was driving away.

"Hey, Richard is just an alias I use sometimes. Nothing to worry about."

"Okay. See you when you get back."

ॐ

We were up for most of the night talking on the balcony and drinking rosé. Our conversation was all about life's ups and downs and how we've navigated things so far. Whenever we had serious conversations, it didn't feel intense but flowed naturally. We both dropped our walls and felt safe enough to be vulnerable and transparent, which only connected us further.

Before Hawaii, I only saw glimpses of his true self, but this trip opened him up. We had been in the talking phase for a while, and that night, things changed. It was a more profound, more authentic version of himself that I was totally into. I could see a future—a bright one.

I grabbed his hand, stopped him mid-conversation, and said, "I just want you to know I don't care about your job. Not in a disrespectful way, but I care about you. Not your access to celebrity, or this high-profile job, I care about you for *you*."

His eyes welled up. "I know!"

"What are your biggest insecurities?" The question popped into my head, and I was curious about his response.

"You always ask such good questions that catch me off-guard." He paused to think. "Honestly, that I am misunderstood."

"Okay, elaborate."

"There's so much going on sometimes. The way that my brain works when I try to communicate how I feel or what I think, people don't often understand me. I walk alone in the world." He shifted and continued, "You know how sometimes you will be like, 'What is *wrong* with you?'"

It was true, I often used this statement when I didn't understand something he was saying or doing. I felt bad, because my goal was usually to better discern who he was as an individual. He continued to explain himself, and I listened. Maybe I needed to go about asking him to explain himself in a different way moving forward. It wasn't my intention to make him feel insecure about himself, but to identify who he was as a man to see if we were a good match.

"Dale, I'm not saying it in a bad way, but more in a funny

way. I think you're quirky, and I like that about you." I hoped my explanation made him feel a little better about the encounters, but my goal was to work on my delivery.

"I know you mean it in a playful way, but many people don't give me the opportunity to dive into that part of myself. They don't want to know that side that is genuine, soft, and vulnerable. Normally, I avoid being this way because I don't want to be targeted for this."

We looked out at how the moon cast shadows about the grounds. We explored each other through words and touch. I learned more about his personality and his mind that night. It felt like he had dropped a lot of weight from his spirit. He said that he felt lighter, and I knew the feeling from years of therapy. It felt good to shed the mask we carry to shield ourselves from the world. I could feel my heartstrings being tugged, and I was excited to possibly be falling in love again.

We finally began to settle down and get ready for bed, but the entire time, we kept talking until we found ourselves cuddled in each other's arms, falling asleep to the lull of our voices. I felt warm and safe wrapped in his arms, surrounded by the smell of his armpits and cologne.

He looked at me and said, "I know I'm shielded and have walls, but I find myself opening up to you more and more. I find myself waking up with thoughts of you and falling asleep in the same mindset."

He had seemed guarded at first, but now I could see his soft and kind side.

# BIRTHDAY IN THE BAY

When I left Hawaii, I forgot some things in our room—my loofah, lotion, and a dress. He texted me a picture of it all with the message:

> "You left a reminder of what made my hotel room
> come to life for the seven days you were here."

It had been a beautiful seven days together, and the deep connections we made during our week together were more memorable than the awkward times. While sitting on the beach, we had made plans for when we would see each other next.

I looked at him and said, "Your birthday is coming up. What are you thinking of doing?"

He shrugged and said, "I don't really do much for my birthday... I'm not much of a birthday person."

"Well, that's going to change! We don't have to have a big hoorah of a party, but birthdays are special, and life should be celebrated."

He joked, "I remember you telling me that a few months ago,

47

and then I saw the video of your fortieth birthday celebration! You're big on birthdays and Christmas, huh?"

"Yep!" I grinned and jumped on top of him. "We can keep it casual-ish but still celebrate."

I had a conference to attend in San Francisco. I suggested he come toward the end of the conference, and I would extend my stay.

We talked daily. We had gone from strangers with the initial excitement of being pursued to a courtship in which I had felt unsure if it would turn into anything more than friendship. Now, we were in a serious... situationship heading toward possibility. A possibility that looked promising. Maybe this unconventional courtship would be my final love story. Then again, I had never felt so conflicted about a relationship before. I usually knew if a relationship was a dead end or not, but he was an anomaly.

I noticed Dale's growth in vulnerability, thoughtfulness, and romance. These qualities infused our relationship with a renewed sense of optimism. He was attentive, ensuring he always faced the entrance at restaurants. Due to his training for his job and past work as a cop, he liked to see the entrance and exit. He eagerly rushed back from work to be with me. Our interactions were filled with cuddles, hugs, and sharing intimate stories from our pasts. His sad puppy-dog eyes sometimes stirred a deep desire within me to embrace him completely.

The idea of sharing our serendipitous story with future generations filled me with hope and determination. After so long without believing in a relationship's potential, I was eager to cherish every moment with Dale.

Even though I was eager, I also felt insecure because, on paper, I didn't seem very appealing. I was divorced with three kids, and society sent messages that I wasn't desirable based on this. While some praised single mothers for their ability to handle multiple responsibilities, others made us feel undesirable because we're seen as having too much baggage. Men were often admired for their adventurous lifestyles, while women were criticized for choosing partners that didn't last. Women were frequently blamed for relationship failures, reinforcing the idea that their value was only in maintaining a relationship with a man.

Single motherhood could be lonely. My days were filled with adult conversations at work, followed by caring for my kids until bedtime. Dale was a refreshing change—a person with whom I could engage in conversations beyond the realm of corporate jargon and elementary school, connecting on a deeper level. His energy and enthusiasm were contagious, and I was intellectually and physically drawn to him.

In a therapy session, I discussed my feelings with my therapist to gain some perspective. I was determined not to rush into a relationship out of loneliness.

"I'm excited... I'm falling for him, but I'm also terrified of being hurt again."

My therapist nodded. "Tell me more about feeling terrified."

We talked through many of the things that terrified me—my parents and their infidelities, how long it took me to get to a place where I was comfortable and ready to date after my divorce, how hard it was to heal from the pain and deception from my ex-boyfriend Clyde, and realizing I was ready to share my life with someone.

CB

The work conference welcome session was over, and now I just had to engage in several days of breakout sessions before I could have my time with Dale afterward. The conference was busy and kept me from thinking too hard about anything else but work, but as we got closer to his arrival, I was distracted. Dale would arrive a day before the last day of the conference, and we would have Wednesday through Saturday together to celebrate him. I had the whole weekend planned. His gift was wrapped and waiting on the bed with a card for him in the hotel room.

As I entered the room, my heart leaped at the sight of Dale. We embraced in our customary bear hug, and I instinctively wrapped my legs around him, feeling an immediate sense of comfort and familiarity. At that moment, the stresses of the workday evaporated, and I was fully present, eager to celebrate and enjoy his company.

He had waited until I was there to open his present, which was a personalized New York Times book for his birthday, with stats from his favorite NBA and NFL teams. There was also a card from Paisley Paper Co. that said, "You're lucky you're cute!" On the inside, I had written a cute note: "Dale Boo! You remind me every day why I kept my heart open. Thank you for being such a beautiful soul. May this next trip around the sun be one for the books. Happy birthday!"

As he read the card, a heartfelt smile spread across his face and his eyes welled up. His vulnerability in that moment spoke volumes, deepening our bond and affirming the intimacy we were building. His reaction made me realize he likely didn't receive many gifts. I felt grateful to be able to bring him joy and be there for him in a meaningful way.

We left to eat and enjoyed a wonderful meal with enlightening conversation. After dinner, we went to a karaoke bar so that he could sing to his heart's delight. We met up with a few of my coworkers, and I slipped the DJ twenty bucks so that he could move up his spot in the line. He chose Lizzo's "It's About Damn Time." He was really entertaining and engaged with the crowd, almost like he was the emcee, host, and entertainer. Every time he did karaoke, I could see him channeling his emotions and tapping into his sensitive side that he couldn't quite display regularly. In some ways, I believed it allowed him to be vulnerable and free under the guise of karaoke. It made sense because he shared that he only did karaoke on the road. It was like this safe space to be free and creative in front of complete strangers. Women sang along in the bar, and it was an all-around great time. Dale was definitely in his element.

We stayed out later than I intended, despite knowing I had to wake up early for the final day of the conference. We went back to the hotel, changed into our bedtime attire, and settled into our regular routine of pillow talk. Eventually, I fell asleep.

In the morning, Dale told me that I had farted several times in my sleep. "They weren't loud or anything. They were cute. I kept thinking to myself, 'I wonder what she ate to make her so gassy?' and then I remembered you had cauliflower. It was the cauliflower! Also, your farts smell like cookies. I lifted the covers to smell."

I was so embarrassed. *What was wrong with him?* He was so quirky that I couldn't be mad. I playfully hit him, and we laughed over it.

Later that day, after my conference activities ended, we walked the Golden Gate Bridge and did a few other tourist activities since he had never been to San Fransisco before. We stopped by Lombard Street, but unfortunately with traffic, we ran out of time to see the house from *Full House*. After seeing the movie *The Bridge*, we stopped and grabbed some coffee, and he researched the movie we'd just seen on IMDb.

After a long day, for dinner we went to Gary Danko, a restaurant a friend had recommended. It turned out that tables were booked for the next three months, so we sat at the bar. The bar only had one seat available, but the hostess and bartender were kind enough to grab another chair and fit us both in. We both enjoyed their three-course menu option. Dale had the seafood bisque and filet with potato gratin and brussels sprouts. I had their arugula salad and horseradish-crusted salmon. He enjoyed the final round of desserts to himself, and since I didn't have much of a sweet tooth, I ordered a glass of rosé. We sat at the bar, resting our tired feet on the railing and letting the steady babble of conversation wash over us.

We were supposed to meet up with one of his coworkers after dinner. Dale pulled out his phone to check for messages, and I saw a text that was stamped eight a.m.

Tisha: "I hope you have a wonderful day! <3"

"Who's Tisha?" I asked. I tried to sound neutral, but maybe a more authentic phrasing would have been, *Who the fuck is that?* Even as I felt my body tense up, braced for dishonesty, I reminded myself—*don't overreact.* It would have been so easy to overreact because of my trust issues, but man, just that emoji made me feel intensely territorial.

He met my eyes and waved his hand as if to say, *nobody.* "Oh, I met her when I was in the Air Force like twenty-five years ago. She's like a little sister to me."

*Like a sister, but not worth mentioning?*

He continued, "We lost touch after the military, but recently, she looked me up and called me out of nowhere just to tell me I was one of the nicest people she'd ever met. So she sends messages every now and again."

I listened quietly to the story and turned it over and over in my mind. It felt off. *If they were so close, why the decades without contact? And what girl is going to call you after all that time apart?*

"She just randomly texted you? How'd she have your number?" Looking up an old friend on Facebook seemed more realistic than having their number out of the blue.

"Well, she actually did search my information on Google and used one of those 'ten bucks to find someone' things."

It just didn't feel like something a platonic friend would do, and an awful lot of work just to say hi. I thought of all my girlfriends who had reached out to exes "out of the blue" to see where things went.

"So yeah, she'll just check in on me to see how I'm doing."

"Huh. So did you date this girl in the past? Did you guys have sex?" My stomach was doing cartwheels like I was about to be sick.

"No, we're just friends," he said so firmly that I wanted to believe him. *Was my mind playing tricks on me?*

Seeing that I was not fully reassured, he said, "I know your ex really did a number on you, but I'm not that guy. It's up to you if you believe me."

I thought of Clyde. One time, he went on a father-and-son trip and sent me a picture of himself with a group of his guy friends and their sons. He was too drunk or dumb to realize what he sent me, because when I zoomed in, I saw two women, one of whom looked like his ex-wife. When I asked him if that was her, he accused me of always looking for a fight, never trusting him, and never allowing him to relax and have a good time. Later, though, I learned that it *was* his ex-wife in that picture, and she wasn't actually his ex-wife. She was his legal wife and was unaware that he was having an affair or even contemplating divorce. Remembering the pain and stress of the way Clyde treated me, it was hard to relax the tension in my body.

Dale's watery eyes helped me feel like he was empathizing rather than dismissing my concerns, though. He was the opposite of Clyde. He was calm and wasn't fighting with me about it or gaslighting me, so I decided I must be overreacting. But still, I wanted the texting to stop.

After the text, I could feel the vibe between Dale and me shift. He looked upset, and I don't like it when people are upset with me, or when something I do or say hurts them. I was a recovering people-pleaser from growing up in a house of lies, and I was working through that in therapy—trying to be okay with having uncomfortable conversations for growth. It made me nervous to feel this way, and then I felt angry that I felt so nervous. I didn't like feeling this way, so I did what I always did—focused on ensuring he was good. That way, I knew in the end that we would be good. It was his birthday, and I didn't want my insecurities to put a damper on the weekend.

Dale was nervous and kept looking at me with pleading eyes to believe him. His friends arrived at the bar, and I didn't want to discuss it in front of them. We were not official, and now I needed clarity before moving any further. I felt like I had to say or do something, though, to get him to relax enough to enjoy his friends. "I want to believe you. We'll talk about it more later."

When we returned to the hotel room, I sat down so that we could discuss Tisha.

"Okay, are you talking to this girl?"

"No, she's just an old friend." It didn't matter how many times he said it. I felt he must be oblivious to her true agenda. This conversation about her stirred up some intense feelings within me. I have lots of close male friends, and that's just not a text I would ever send.

"That's just Tisha's Southern charm. I don't bother to text her back." He showed me the text chain and how he hadn't responded.

We sat in silence while I gathered the rest of my thoughts. His response had given me a little reassurance, but it wasn't enough. "We're not official, so at this point, I can't be upset, but I'm not about to be out in these streets holding hands and kissing and traveling with you when you got other shit going on."

"Tisha means nothing to me." Tears welled up in his eyes.

My body language showed that I was not vibing well. We took

a break from our heavy conversation to get ready for bed, and before I could relax and lie down for the night, I decided to officially put the conversation to rest.

"I need you to know that I really like you. I think you're an amazing person with a beautiful soul. Even if things don't work out between us, I want us to remain friends." I adjusted myself to make sure we had complete eye contact. "But I will not be with someone who's dating other people. You can just let me know if that is what you prefer so we can end this amicably."

Dale began to cry.

"I can't be flying around the world without commitment. So if this is not going to be much more than casual dating or friendship, I can't do it. I don't move like this."

The tears continued to stream down his face. "I just never felt like this before, especially so soon."

Another silence filled the room while he tried to compose himself.

"You want to go together?" he sheepishly asked.

The innocence of the request made me smile. He knew how to take a moment and divert it in a direction that would tie my heart in knots. I played it off. "Shut up." I blushed and tried to forget what he had just said.

"No, for real." He grabbed my hand and kissed it. I could see that he was serious and considered the question. "I want you in my life. I'm falling really hard for you. I want you to be my girlfriend. So will you?"

"Do you feel pressured to say that to me?"

"No, I'm just so guarded all the time. So maybe you're feeling a little of that, and I don't want you to. I want to articulate better how I feel about you. I want you in my life. So, will you be my girlfriend?"

He seemed to be intentionally putting in the effort necessary to create a good thing between us. I thought carefully about it, and it didn't feel like he was just doing things to appease me but that he genuinely wanted me around. It was the first time I had heard him state what I could feel in our everyday interactions. He was a project in some ways—I could tell he didn't understand what I was really getting at about Tisha. But it wasn't anything I couldn't handle, and every relationship had things that each person would have to work on to improve the relationship.

I especially enjoyed how Dale did his best to remain connected to me. It felt like he did more than just listen to my words; he felt my energy, and if he felt a shift, he would adjust himself to meet me where I was. I'd never experienced that kind of attentiveness in other relationships. What Dale and I had felt more natural and rooted in truth and vulnerability. He desired me, and that felt exhilarating. To be wanted by another was the ultimate high. No rosé necessary!

"Yeah, I'll be your girlfriend, but there's something I need you to do for me."

"What's that?"

"I need you to let Tisha know that you have someone in your life now and her texts are no longer appropriate."

He looked at me, and we sealed the promise with a kiss. I lay back in his arms for the first time that night, and we lay in silence for several minutes. We had made it official. It felt good to be starting something new and promising.

"When you said if we don't work out, you still want to be friends. Did you mean that?"

"Yes, I do mean it," I replied. He held me tightly like he did when we first saw each other after weeks apart. I felt safe in his arms, ready to explore the next level of our budding relationship.

☾

The next day, he got up early to walk to the nearest Starbucks to grab my coffee, but instead, I suggested we watch the last two episodes of *From Scratch* that we had been binge-watching. I bawled when Lino died, and the last episode had me ugly crying. He squeezed me as we were lying in bed and joking about Lino's bad bald cap. We chatted about the day ahead of us while lying in each other's arms, and then he abruptly said, "Get up! I want you to sit on my face!"

With his strong arms, he picked me up and threw my body on top of his face, lifting my camisole nightgown.

55

"Keep your eyes open to watch yourself in the mirror," he said.

The intensity was wild. He was holding tight to my butt and the second I orgasmed he threw me on my bed for intercourse. He was on top of me and holding my hips back while sucking my toes. I hadn't ever had this type of sexual chemistry, comfort, and connection with anyone. He was a big pleaser, always watching to see my reactions and go deeper.

# THE NEW YEAR

Going into the New Year with a new relationship was just what I needed. It was refreshing to be affirmed that through therapy and self-discovery, I was finding myself on a different relational footing that was more secure than my past relationships and felt like a pathway to avoid the kind of trauma I'd experienced in childhood. I had found a man who was considerate of my feelings and took into account that we had differences that complemented and challenged each other. I was ready to head back to Hawaii to see my man.

The week before I was supposed to arrive in Hawaii, I noticed that every time I talked to Dale, he was running around doing errands. He'd never been at the mall so much, almost daily. I found it strange but chalked it up to his quirkiness.

I flew in on December twenty-seventh, ready to make some memories. I had gotten Dale three gifts—an experience, a memento, and something he needed. When we first arrived at the hotel, we immediately exchanged gifts.

Dale opened his gifts first. He loved the shirts I'd picked out. At a bar a few weeks before, he had commented that he liked these shirts on another guy with a similar build, and I thought they would look good on him, so I found them. I also gave him the NCAA University of Michigan football history book, which I'd intended to be a birthday gift, but it had been delivered late. The experience gift was a yacht adventure day for us to go on together. He loved them all. His reaction alone was enough to get me through the rest of the trip.

His gifts to me were a spa day and a Bally crossbody style purse, a brand he loved and had been adamant about me trying. The last box was the most thoughtful and best gift ever. He had found my favorite perfume, Tom Ford Noir, which had been recently discontinued. I couldn't find a bottle anywhere, but he managed to scrounge up one last bottle. I was beyond words at the grand gesture.

He proceeded to tell me the story of how, after I had told him that he needed to get his last whiffs because it was all I had, he took a picture of the bottle. He had gone to every mall he could searching for it. At every store, they told him that it had been discontinued.

"I went to one last store, and the lady returned with the last bottle. She said, 'This bottle must have been meant for you. I've looked before for other customers. I only looked to be thorough enough to tell you we didn't have any more with confidence. But look at what I have instead!' I've never been so happy to see a bottle of perfume."

I felt the same way as I held it in my arms. I was going to ration this stuff.

"I told her, 'Give me this bottle! She's been wearing this same scent for five years,' and she said, 'You better marry this girl!'"

I gave a high-pitched scream of excitement and grabbed onto the man I cherished, so thankful that he put in so much effort to make me happy. This relationship was beginning to feel like a fairy tale compared to my past experiences. I jumped up and down all over him in a frenzy. It was a moment of pride for him; I could see it in his stance. My reaction helped to give him a big pat on his back for a job well done. My man had gone out of his way for me, creating this moment. I was falling for this guy hard. It felt amazing to be heard by a man who would act on my words.

The next day, we used certificates I had purchased for a yacht adventure to swim with the turtles. We set out to sail the beautiful Hawaiian waves. It seemed like a great way to spend our time together and try something new together. I extended an invite to a few of his coworkers to join us on the sunset boat ride. We boarded the boat for a nature adventure. The waters were very violent, with sharp ups and downs. We swam with the turtles, which I didn't enjoy as much as I expected to. They were way bigger than I thought they would be, and I was freaked out by them. I thought we would have a bougie and leisure experience, but it was nothing like that. The salt water was getting on my hair and in my mouth, and after just a few minutes, I was over the whole experience.

The aggressive boat ride made Dale seasick. As we lay on the nets on the front of the fifty-two-foot classic Hawaiian catamaran, I asked Dale how he was doing.

"I'm feeling a little nauseous," he whispered before leaning over to barf through one of the holes in the net. I felt so bad for him.

"Don't look!" he said.

"What do you mean, 'Don't look?' You're right in front of me. Besides, I need to help you, silly."

I told the captain what was happening and asked if he had any Dramamine. He didn't, so I grabbed some water and crackers and suggested we return to the dock. As we headed slowly back to land, the sun was setting. I think at that moment, Dale finally understood my infatuation with sunsets. He stared at the colors and kept his eyes on the water. It was a special way to end the day.

He wasn't fully better but looked less queasy. He put his hand on my leg and asked one of the yacht attendees to take some pictures of us together. He tried to muscle through the motion sickness, but we could see in the pictures that he didn't feel well. Once we got closer to the dock, he threw up again. I felt so bad.

For the next few days, we did our normal things. He worked, and we went with the flow during our time together. We went out to eat at a new spot he had found called the Pupu House. Pupu meant appetizers in Hawaiian. It had a playful tiki bar vibe, and the food was delicious. Everything was fresh—the chicken tacos, coconut shrimp, edamame, and the ribs—it all just melted in our mouths. It was the perfect balance of sweet and savory for us. We ate so much that we were in a food coma afterward.

We left the Pupu House and went for a walk before making our way to karaoke. I loved watching him do karaoke. He looked so free and did shout-outs to me, like saying "I'm the luckiest man in the world" while pointing at me. He knew I was often recording him. He was becoming more vulnerable and open as we got closer. He was so into karaoke that recently when he overheard me singing the Donna Lewis song "I Love You Always Forever," I promised him if he learned the song, I'd perform it with him one day. So he started trying to learn the beat and lyrics to make sure he could groove to it for one of our upcoming karaoke sessions.

We planned our New Year's Eve. We saw this beautiful glass restaurant overlooking the beach during our boat tour and thought it would be a great view to see the fireworks at midnight. He called to see about reservations, but they were completely booked, so we decided on RumFire for dinner. It was another beautifully decorated restaurant with a view of the ocean, large windows, a patio, and a variety of healthy options that I appreciated.

We got to the restaurant around seven, and when Dale gave him his number for the table reservation, the host recognized the Detroit area code. He made sure we received one of the best tables with a great view of the ocean and the upcoming fireworks. The host had exuberant energy that was bold and carefree. He took charge and told us, "I'm *your* guy." The spot that he chose for us gave a perfect view of the sunset while we dined, and he seated another couple of Detroiters next to us so that we had people to talk with.

Every New Year's Eve since I could remember, my family presented their rose and thorn of the year. The rose was the highlight of the year, and the thorn was something that didn't go so well. I held on to this tradition and presented Dale with the question.

"What was your rose and thorn for the year?"

"You love asking introspective questions." He thought a little more and answered, "My rose is that my father is still alive, but the thorn is... recognizing his old age, and that his days are numbered."

He shared about his most recent visit with his father and how his father didn't have much longer in this world. His father struggled to do the simplest things, and accidental falls were a danger. His dad needed a lot of assistance and used a walker to get around.

"Soon I'll be parentless." Tears welled up in his eyes and fell down his cheeks. I reached across the table to hold his hands, listening intently and stroking his hand to let him know that I was there for him.

"Maybe you could try to go home to visit him more often while he's still here?" I suggested. "Have I told you about my grandmother?"

"No... what happened?"

"Well, my grandmother had just been discharged from the hospital and we knew she didn't have much time left. My grandmother seemed to have nine lives, though—she survived so much in her final years that the doctors were always amazed she was still alive. She made it through strokes, heart attacks, blood clots, you name it. That week, I had a work trip to Seattle from Sunday to Thursday. I made it home Thursday evening and had intended to go see my grandmother right away, but I was exhausted. My daughter was seven months old at the time, and all I wanted to do was be with her and sleep in my own bed."

"Understandable," Dale said.

"So I planned to see my grandmother on Friday after picking my daughter up from daycare. On the way to daycare, twenty minutes before my visit, I got a call from my mother that my grandmother had died. I broke down. I regretted that decision for so long and held on to a lot of guilt. We have to make time for our family, especially our elders." I told him, "You're loved. Stop trying to move through life so guarded. Make more time to be with your dad so that if and when the day comes—because we never know who will go first—you have no regrets." I figured that if he saw his father more, he could feel more connected to him for whatever time his father had left.

"What is it about you that has me in tears all the time? I've cried more with you than I have cried in the last twenty-five years. I don't think I cried this hard at my mom's funeral." He wiped his face. "I gotta stop crying before these people think you're beating me."

Of course he made light of a heavy moment, but it was understandable to break the heaviness of the moment.

"Why are you like this?" he asked.

"I just want and need a deep connection with my partner."

We kept talking late into the night, totally immersed in each other. We were cultivating the kind of solid communication foundation I had always yearned for. The energy became more light-hearted as the night wore on. We were back to belly laughs, and he did his best to make me laugh. His eyes were no longer low and sad, but eager, wide, alert, and engaging.

Dale always had a story. "Did I ever tell you about Sharon, a girl I dated in my twenties?"

"No."

"Well, here's another story for you... we used to call her Lexus because that's all she drove, but her real name is Sharon."

I listened with intent. He always had such good stories.

"I wouldn't even say that we were dating—we were talking, but she became crazy."

"What made you think she was crazy?"

"I was a cop back then, and she would call me, and if I didn't answer, she'd call back-to-back. A lot of times, I would be on a job at some incident, so I couldn't talk. Obviously, I'd plan to call her back, but it usually wasn't fast enough for her. Then I would get these angry voicemails from her accusing me of cheating, ignoring her... she threw every accusation my way." Dale's elevated story-telling voice sounded like Katt Williams telling a story.

"I kept pleading with her to calm down and reminding her that I was working and would call her back. She was so up and down with her emotions. Like one time we were out to dinner, and the waitress messed up her order. I've never seen someone snap and be so angry to a waitress because they forgot to substitute eggs for extra hashbrowns. It was embarrassing. At one point it got so bad that I bluntly asked her if she was taking meds."

"Like for mental illness?"

"Yeah! Anyway, we stopped talking shortly after that, but the craziest thing happened on New Year's Eve. A few times she wanted to have sex, and I didn't have a condom on me, so on New Year's Eve, I stopped by the store on the way to her place and bought some. We're hanging out in her bedroom and she asks if I brought condoms. I say, 'Yes,' she asks where they are, and I show her the box. She says, 'Gimme that!' yanks the box out of my hand, and leaves the room. So I'm lying there, mentally prepared to do this, and minutes go by. I get up to see what the hell is going on, and I found her ass in the bathroom poking holes—" He motioned poking holes.

I squawked, "What did you say?"

"Well, I scream, 'Sharon!' She freezes and looks at me with the needle still in her hand."

I repeated, "What did you say!"

"I yelled her name and told her to throw it away!" He replied.

"Tell me you didn't go back and fuck her?" I asked.

"I mean... I was in my twenties. I just got a new condom."

I was baffled. "You've gotta be kidding. Shut—the—fuck—up!"

Dale paused and looked at me with glazed eyes and vacant anger. I had never seen him look like that before. He leaned forward on the high-top stool and asked, "Are you drunk?"

The monotone and aggressive cadence took me back. I tried to figure out where the question had come from. We'd been together all night, so he had seen what I'd had to drink. We'd each had two glasses of wine, so I definitely wasn't drunk. I adjusted in my seat.

"What?"

*Had I heard him correctly? Maybe I was mistaken.* It felt like a confusing dream. His eyes were focused on me but glossed over. He seemed to shake it off as if he had a chill and began to blink.

"Never mind," he said.

"No, what was that?" I was a little spooked.

"Nothing, never mind."

I felt uneasy. "Are you upset with me?" I began to fish for logical explanations for what had occurred. "You just looked at me hella crazy, so I want to know what that was about."

I was focused on finding an answer and not letting him wiggle away from a response. I was invested in this relationship and wanted to know what I could do to help him through whatever was happening.

He took a deep breath and began. "I don't know if I told you this story. It was when I was still a police officer. I was supposed to pick up my son from daycare. He was about eighteen months old at the time. Well, I got called on a case, so I called the daycare provider to tell them I would be late. They let me know that it was okay. I finished up work and went to pick him up. When I got home, my wife was furious and went off on me. She lost her shit, saying stuff like, 'You gotta be fucking kidding me? You must be fucking stupid, just a fucking idiot! Why would you do some stupid shit like leave our son there?' Going on and on, berating me and yelling. I got upset and said, 'Fuck this shit.' Our son began crying, and I grabbed my keys and left the house. I went to grab a drink and calm down." His body was tense and tight at first, but his shoulders looked more relaxed as he went on to tell the story, almost like a slight weight was lifted. His voice was steady, not like his storytelling voice, but almost like an investigative debrief.

I felt bad for pressing him. Some stories seemed to really bring up his insecurities, and this was clearly one of them. I could see the connection between what I had said and the dialogue in the story to some degree, but we always joked around like this. I hadn't been hostile—I'd said those words in a joking manner. And I never called him any demeaning names. *Do we need to limit how we joke with each other now?* I wanted to be respectful of his triggers and the boundaries surrounding them.

"I was joking around with you."

"I know. Don't worry about it." He grabbed my hand and looked me lovingly in the eyes. "It just felt like when she called me stupid. It was a connection I made. I'm sorry. It had nothing to do with you. It's me. I need to own it. It has nothing to do with you."

I still felt terrible. He had shared how tumultuous and contentious their relationship was. I felt like I needed to be softer with him even though he hadn't requested it. I had thought we knew each other well enough for him to know I didn't mean any harm.

After the volatile conversation, it felt awkward. I appreciated the other couple from Detroit being seated near us as an opportunity to clear the air. We focused the conversation outside of ourselves and our mixed emotions. They were a cute older Black couple, probably in their late sixties, who were happy to be on vacation. The wife and I connected over both being from the East Side of Detroit. She went to the same high school as my aunts, so we tried to figure out if they knew each other. The men started talking about directions and old historical sites throughout the city of Detroit, what was there now and what was no longer there, where they worked, and what they did. The older gentleman was excited to find out Dale was a Secret Service agent assigned to the Obama detail.

It was 9:30 by the time we checked the time. We had already had dinner and drinks but still had a long way to go to bring in the new year at midnight. Honestly, both of us were ready to take a nap. We were trying to figure out if we would go back to the hotel and call it a night, or power through to midnight. Dale was adamant that I should see the fireworks, so we stayed. We ordered some french fries to share and a couple more cocktails to keep things going, but we were tired. By the time eleven came around, Dale's eyes were bloodshot. He had been up all day and would have to get up early for work again tomorrow.

As midnight finally approached, the restaurant staff handed out hats and little accessories for us to bring in the new year. We stood with the older couple, counting down with excitement. Dale grabbed my waist and pulled me closer as we all screamed "Ten, nine, eight..." As soon as we got to "one!" he pulled me in. I grabbed the back of his head, and we kissed. I had the biggest smile on my face, and we wished each other, "Happy New Year!" *This year will be so much better,* I thought, watching the fireworks and cheering with the crowd.

Everyone else was ready to turn up, but we were prepared to turn down and get some rest. Once the theatrics in the sky were over, we headed back to our room. It had been a long, emotional day of ups and downs.

In the hotel room, it was a relief to change into my nightgown.

We made sure the curtains were all the way closed to keep the lights from the other high-rise hotels from shining in and waking us up, and then curled up in bed. I was the little spoon, and he was the big spoon.

"Can you turn the temperature a bit warmer?" He ran hotter than me, so he'd often have the AC set to sixty-nine degrees, and I'd wake up in the middle of the night freezing and get up to adjust the temperature.

"Sure." He adjusted the thermostat, and we went to sleep.

# ABSOLUTELY SURPRISED

On FaceTime one night, I asked Dale, "How would you feel if your ex got remarried or introduced someone to your son?"

"Oh, I'd be fine with it, as long as my son didn't call the other guy Dad."

"I'm a bit careful on this. My kids get attached quickly when it comes to my friends and family. They have big hearts, they love big, and remember everything—even our second au pair." I'd seen my girlfriends have revolving doors of boyfriends around their kids, and it concerned me. I had childhood traumas associated with bringing men around children. Unless we were about to start engagement ring shopping, there was no reason for my kids to know he existed.

I didn't say this to Dale, but when I was younger, my mother dated men while my dad was away. Guys would come around, and it would hurt my heart. I pictured my mom as the villain in the family's love story, although I only knew what I could see. I didn't trust these men or like them. I could still remember the whites of their eyes, the yellow of their teeth, and the smell of Newports left behind on everything they touched. I had no idea that my father was creating another family while he was in Liberia. All I knew was what my mother was doing at the time, so I promised myself that if I ever had kids of my own, I would only show them serious candidates.

Dale said, "I got you—whenever you're ready."

I had two important birthdays coming up—my son's and my good friend Stella's. I told Dale I wasn't quite ready for him to meet my kids yet, but he kept asking about Stella's birthday party, so I sent him the flyer invitation. He wanted to see how we did things. He was surprised by the level of detail and planning involved. The invitation called for it to be a dress-to-impress event.

"You guys are a bit over the top in celebrating yourselves!" he said.

I responded, "Who will if we don't?"

He had known about Stella's birthday bash for a while, and he wanted to be my date at her party without overlapping with my son's birthday celebration.

Dale reached out to Stella through Facebook, alerting her that he wanted to surprise me by showing up as my date to her party. He told her that he had been asking me a lot of questions about Minneapolis but didn't think I was connecting the dots. I wasn't—I didn't think he was crazy enough to just pop up on me like that. I found all his questions about the weather, airport, delays, and cancellations strange. Meanwhile, Dale told Stella to keep it a secret, and she held his confidence for as long as she could.

"What's up with all of these questions?"

"You know me. I'm just weird like that. I want to know things, that's all." He tried to soothe me. It didn't work. My brain began working in a thousand ways, and since it was that time of the month, my hormones were raging.

I met up with Stella at a restaurant called Boulevard. We were both hormonal and not feeling well. She was craving steak and dessert, and I wanted banana apple bread with ice cream. Both of us were just bitching and bleeding. We had a couple margaritas, and Dale was texting me. I sent him a text telling him that I missed him, and he responded with hearts. My emotions were erratic and without apparent cause, leading me to feel unexpectedly slighted. I ended up calling him and venting my frustration before impulsively passing the phone to Stella.

I found her end of the conversation a little suspect. I finally connected the dots and had mixed emotions about the possibility of him surprising me. I didn't like surprises. If this man was coming to see me, I needed time to prepare for his arrival—get waxed, hair done, nails refreshed, and all that good stuff.

She passed the phone back to me, and I began to question him hard.

"Why do you keep asking questions about Minnesota? Specifically, why are you asking questions like 'Is MSP the main airport?' and 'How frequently are there flight delays and cancellations in Minnesota?' and 'How frequently do you visit the Mall of America?'"

He was evasive and didn't really answer my questions. Finally, I blurted out, "Babe! You know those toes that you like to suck on? Well, they need a pedicure, so if you're coming, I need to get shit scheduled. Don't just pop up like that!"

He laughed and admitted that he had reached out to his travel coordinator to book a hotel room at the JW Marriott at the MOA. He planned on staying there for two days and wanted to see the smile and shock on my face as he walked into Stella's party.

I was shocked, excited, and ready to drop the call so I could make all the appointments to be ready for his arrival. I was happy that he made the effort to surprise me, but I was even more delighted that he told me beforehand. Now, he didn't have to roam around Minneapolis for a whole day and a half trying to entertain himself; we could spend it together.

I made arrangements for the kids to go to their dad's for the weekend, and I made sure he knew to call if he needed to stop by for anything. I had my cleaning lady come that Thursday instead of her usual Monday so that my house wasn't in complete disarray, and I did everything on my beautifying list.

I had an opportunity to personally show Dale around my city. Minneapolis in January was not the prettiest sight. It was brown, cold, and usually overcast. Instead of him getting a hotel as he had intended, he stayed at my place. It was so nice having him there. It was everyday living. I cooked him lunches and dinners. It was his first opportunity to see my daily life. We went out to dinner one night, but I enjoyed coming home and preparing a meal. It felt like we actually lived together for a few days. It felt perfect. Our relationship up to this point was mostly visits at hotels, but now we were in my home, where I felt more relaxed and calmer. In my own space, I felt free to be me. I didn't have to guess because everything was mine and where I left it last. It was an area where I could let down my hair, and now I was with a man and could relax and just be me.

One afternoon, I busied myself preparing a salad. A few minutes later, Dale joined me in the kitchen, observing me skillfully chopping the vegetables and mixing the dressing from scratch. Quietly, he approached from behind and enveloped me in a warm, reassuring hug.

"I see why it takes you so long to call me back when you say you're making a salad."

We sat down at the island to eat and chat.

"This is actually good," he exclaimed. "You can make this for us when we're old and gray." The sentiment did not escape me. I smiled and gave him a kiss on the lips, biting his full bottom lip. I was starting to feel like I had found my person.

My ex-boyfriend, Clyde, had been too damaged to realize he was dragging me through the mud. Dale, though, felt like a breath of fresh air. He seemed more aware of his faults and more receptive to responding to feedback and changing. His ability to dig deeper when I asked him to helped me feel secure that this relationship was a positive in my life. Despite our growing pains, the problems were addressed, and we worked through them together.

I continued to talk through my issues and concerns about our relationship with my therapist. Dale felt like a workable project. Some things needed to be dealt with for this relationship to go the distance, but he was committed to making us work, as was I. I found him attractive, intelligent, protective, and funny. Every moment Dale and I spent together, I felt the shadows slowly lift to reveal more. I was intrigued by him and his core. He was intentional with me; neither my marriage nor my last dating relationship had felt so deliberate.

It was the first time I was able to drop my insecurities. He revealed his broken pieces and allowed me to be his safe space. I love being a safe space for others, mainly because I lacked it as a child. My parents did not have the best relationship. After my divorce, I did a lot of unpacking myself. In my journey to self-discovery, I learned that my first example of love was dysfunctional. In my parents' marriage, there were multiple affairs, fighting, and financial and emotional abuse. It was not an example of what was ideal.

Looking back at the other relationships I was exposed to as a child, there wasn't really anything healthy to absorb. My grandparents had separate rooms and were not close. To spend time with them, we had to do so in their individual rooms. I would go to my grandfather's room to watch *Sanford and Son*, then go to my grandmother's room to watch *Days of Our Lives*. This was my normal. Grandpa's room had blue walls and wood furniture and smelled like Old Spice. He was always sitting at the head of the bed watching *Sanford and Son*. His laugh was infectious, and Fred Sanford always had him cracking up. Grandpa was missing a few teeth but didn't care—his smile was as big as the moon. Grammy's room was the exact opposite. She had this big red round bed that they had moved down from the attic. My cousins and I would sleep on it when we had sleepovers. For some reason, even though their rooms were separated by a four-foot hallway, her room smelled like mothballs. The scent was so strong that even my Grandpa's Old Spice never made its way to her room.

I have a brother who is nine months younger than me. It wasn't until I was about seven that I realized we didn't have the same mother. I heard my father tell him to pack his things to go to his mother's house for the summer. When I heard that, I put two and two together.

When my grandfather was murdered during the Liberian war, my father went back to Liberia to rescue other family members and get them to safety. He was gone for four years. We thought my father was being held captive and not able to get home because of the war.

I also grew up without having a lot of money. We lived in the projects, and a community of people helped to raise me. But my original source of love, support, and guidance was not strong. As I got older, I learned about the transgressions of both my parents. My parents were primarily concerned with themselves and less about their children, or at least that was how it sometimes felt. We kids were wrapped in their chaos.

When I was eleven, my mother became unable to care for us due to back surgery. My mom couldn't walk up the stairs, so she slept on the floor of our living room on a pile of blankets and pillows for nearly six months.

As the oldest, it fell to me to take care of my siblings and run the household. I took on cooking, cleaning, and the logistics of getting my little sister to preschool every day. It went beyond typical big sister duties. Instead of recess activities with my friends, I'd sit at the fence with my little sister because she would cry the entire time.

When my dad returned, he brought a child from his new family in Liberia with him. Apparently he had made a whole new family in Liberia during his years there, and this was my half-sibling. Shortly after, we packed up and moved twelve hours away to a predominantly white suburb in Plymouth, Minnesota. He said it was for a new job, but it seemed like he was running away from my mother's family and their judgment. I had no say, so my whole life was upended, and I felt alone and voiceless. Trust is hard to earn with me.

Dale gained my trust through persistence, vulnerability, and our chemistry. I was able to revert to the child that needed protection, love, and care, which felt healing. He provided all that and more.

At Stella's party, Dale had a chance to meet and socialize with my friends. All my good friends waited eagerly to introduce themselves to him, almost like they were ready to interview him. People were drawn to him. They wanted to know who this big, tall Black man was. He was my man, and I was proud to show him off. My girlfriends asked him a million questions because they knew my previous relationship hadn't gone so well. My girls didn't want me dating another dud, so they were proactive about getting to know him. They were in his grill, getting all the nitty-gritty; they even asked how to spell his middle name. One of my friends asked about the details and demands of his job. He kept looking around, and she asked what he was preoccupied with while she was talking with him. He admitted that he was looking at the fire suppression supplies and nearest exit strategies. It gave my friends a good laugh.

Dale was attentive to my friends and ensured that none of us ever had an empty drink. Later that night, he got on stage and sang karaoke enthusiastically like he was on stage at his concert, throwing out a few birthday shoutouts to Stella as well. He sang his go-to, Lit's "My Own Worst Enemy," with Stella, the karaoke queen.

He usually enjoyed giving an outstanding performance but felt overshadowed by someone who followed behind him and sang a Michael Jackson song. He felt the other performer captured more of the audience's attention than he had. After the guy sang, Dale came to where I was sitting and voiced his disappointment in a way that seemed cute and childlike.

"I'd never think to sing that song for karaoke. Did you see how he got the crowd going?" he said.

"It was a great song, but it was also the energy the singer brought to the song."

He looked at me, inspired. "I need to add that to my rotation!" He did add that song to his rotation, beginning to work on his beat the next day.

We had a really good time at the party, and he seemed to fit in well. I felt excited to have someone in my life who I didn't feel ashamed of, who I could be out and about with. Finally, I had a man who didn't wander off and do his own thing but would find me to ensure I was good and didn't need anything. I felt warm and happy envisioning our life if this continued. We talked more about our relationship and where we thought we were headed, and I felt secure that we were on the same page.

CB

The day came for him to leave. As I turned on the ignition, a few lights on my dashboard came on.

"Why do you have all those lights on in your car?" he asked.

"I don't know. I need to get an oil change."

"Yeah, and you need your tire pressure checked, you need gas..." he continued with a laundry list of other things that needed to be taken care of. My car was always one area of my life where I was irresponsible. We went to get most of the things taken care of, like gas and tire pressure, but he made me promise to take care of the rest. I could see the worry on his face, and I promised to do it so he wouldn't have to worry.

When we pulled up to the airport, he was still holding tightly to my hand as he had the whole car ride. It felt good. We exited the car, and he retrieved his bags from the trunk. I didn't want him to leave, but I understood the dynamic of our relationship. Plus, I knew I would be seeing him soon enough. I could be patient. Dale pulled me in close and gave me a big hug and long kiss. He looked into my eyes for what felt like an eternity.

"I need you to know that I care about you deeply."

"Promise?" I asked.

"I promise, I care for you deeply."

We kissed again.

"I'll call you when I get to Detroit."

I watched his tall figure and bald head disappear into the bustling airport crowd, pulling his oversized suitcase and carrying his suit garment bag.

# VALENTINE'S DAY

A few weeks later, Dale flew home to see his father, son, and friends. I was excited for him and glad that he was acting on my advice and making a concerted effort to be there for his family. We talked a little, and then he went to hang out with his friends.

The next day, though, he deviated from our regular routine and didn't call or text me in the morning like he had been doing since the day we met. I knew he'd had guy time the previous night and was probably up late, so I didn't think too much of it. I didn't jump to any conclusions, but when it got to be almost two o'clock and still there was no word, I began to worry. I sent him a text saying that I hoped he was having a good time with his family and to please check in with me. By seven that evening, I was getting annoyed that he hadn't even bothered to respond to my text.

I was wondering if the shoe was starting to drop right after we made things official. I wasn't prepared for him to be so dismissive of me. I texted again, and he responded by finally calling me, but I was already peeved by then. He made it seem like it was no big deal and told me he had gotten distracted. I had only needed a simple text, and his excuses made it worse. After going back and forth about how I respected his time with his family but that he didn't just get to disappear for twenty-four hours and ignore my texts, I decided to drop it.

"Let me step outside," he said.

"No, I know you're with the boys, and I don't want you to step out. You don't need to be outside on the phone making it look like we are fighting. Just call me when you're driving home."

Later, when we spoke, I told him I felt disrespected. We weren't married, but if that was how he handled communication when he was with his friends, I no longer wanted to participate in this relationship. His actions affected me. It was something I needed to process to make sure I wasn't projecting or allowing my past to creep into our relationship. I couldn't help but ask myself if he had become too comfortable.

I questioned myself—*was I overreacting?* I remembered that previously when he was away, he was intentional about keeping in touch. When he was in Louisiana with his brothers and father, he would call with cute check-ins. One time, he called me, and I could tell he was a little buzzed. When he heard the Second Line celebration off in the distance, he expressed his excitement and how he'd never seen it in person. I urged him to go experience it, but he said didn't want to get off the phone with me. I pushed him to find it, and he walked all around trying to find them.

Another time, he went to Detroit for the weekend and sent me a text that said "Miss your ass!" out of the blue.

This was early on when we weren't even official. I responded, "I kinda needed to hear that. Miss you too."

The next day he asked me, "What was the 'kinda needed that' response about last night, babycakes?"

I told him, "Get out of your head."

He said, "You know I can't help it."

I told him that in that moment, I was just really missing him and sometimes I needed to hear from his softer side.

He relaxed, "You soften me up more and more by the day."

So this trip felt different, and because of my past, it threw me back into my relationship with Clyde.

"If this is an indication of things to come, then I want no part in it," I told Dale.

"Wow, I didn't think we would be having a conversation about ending things. I'm really caught off-guard. I don't want to throw the baby out with the bath water. I don't want to talk to you while you're upset. Can we sit on this and then talk about it in the morning?"

"Sure." I felt deflated. I had said all that I could say and was getting nowhere anyway. Putting a pin in it would also give me a chance to gather my thoughts and gain more clarity on the situation.

I hoped we could also find our way through this, but I didn't feel hopeful. If I had to let him go, now would be the time. I was not compromising my expectations to be in a relationship with him. He would have to adjust or let go. I needed to remain vigilant so that I could stay comfortable and safe within our relationship. My goal was to find something that served me; as much as I compromised and adjusted, I wanted the same from my next long-term partner in return.

ભ

Dale called me bright and early the next morning. "Hey, babe. I didn't get much sleep last night. I want to apologize again. I don't want to lose you, and I'm sorry for taking you for granted."

I listened intently. He told me that he worried that his selfish nature would end up hurting me. People assumed he didn't care, and more times than not, that assumption was spot on.

"With you, that's really not the case. I care about you so much and I'm willing to put in the work."

Despite encountering another significant challenge, his many admirable qualities shone through. We navigated through our disagreements and continued our relationship. Holding my ground, I saw his commitment to making things work affirm my significance in his life.

I remembered one evening a few weeks earlier, when we were chatting on FaceTime, Dale had recounted a memory of an incident where he and a friend were gearing up for an evening out. His friend suddenly gripped his chest, breathless and overwhelmed, convinced he was having a heart attack. He pleaded with Dale to dial 911.

"I looked over to him and he was on the floor grabbing his chest. He kept asking me to call 911."

"Did you help him?" I asked.

"No. I told to him get it together and that he was fine, let's go." His tone felt indifferent and dismissive.

"Never do that again!" I said, imagining how he might respond if I ever had a panic attack around him. "Even if it wasn't a heart attack, panic attacks are a horrible thing to experience. It can be hard to calm your mind down. I've been to urgent care twice for them. It's debilitating."

"Really? Damn. Well, it seemed like he was overreacting."

I had shared with him some of my own stories of anxiety and moments when I had panic attacks. I'd experienced quite a few panic attacks in the last decade or so. Some I could manage on my own, and others required medication. I'd called my mom, stepdad, and older cousin to come watch the kids as I tried to do my breath work and process. One time, my stepdad had to carry me from my bedroom to the car and drive me to urgent care, where I found out it was a panic attack that felt like a heart attack. I was concerned with how dismissive Dale was with his friend's anxiety and how he would respond to me if one were to happen while we were together. *What would I want him to do?* But I didn't want to give up on the relationship.

I pulled myself back from my memories of previous conversations. Dale was still talking about our conflict.

"I've always said, I am who I am. When you said those things last night, it struck a chord with me. I've never had anyone like you in my life. Our conversations make me think about my actions, how I treat people, and how I want to treat you. I barely slept last night thinking about everything. I'm not okay with not having you in my life."

Slowly, I began to hear the man I had fallen for come back to me.

"I'm willing to put in the work. I don't want to lose you," he said.

My tense shoulders began to relax.

"The fact that I was able to tell you that I care about you deeply so freely really caught me by surprise." There was a long pause before he said, "Coco, I'm in love with you." I could hear him tearing up, and my heartstrings were all entangled again.

"I love you, too," I confessed. It felt good to say those words. I meant them wholeheartedly and found myself profoundly affected by his admission. We had fallen together, and it felt liberating.

&#8478;

His profession of his love for me and his willingness to work on his selfishness felt like a great way to go into the Valentine's Day holiday. We talked about how I didn't have big expectations for Valentine's Day, and I knew he had to work.

However, while I was packing for my conference in Vegas, I could feel a shift in his energy; it had dropped significantly. We were talking on the phone, and he was crying and sharing his unsettled feelings with me. He lost the pep in his voice and sounded very down, like he was struggling. I kept asking him what was wrong. He seemed off and emotionally struggling.

Finally, he asked, "Could you come out to Hawaii?"

Before I left for my Vegas conference, I set up the kids to stay with my mother. Dale told me he really needed me by his side. I could hear it in his voice, which seemed to worsen as the days passed. He booked my flight for Friday morning after the conference was over.

"We can watch the Super Bowl together," he said.

I wanted to show up for him. When I looked back over my conference schedule, I saw that I could make it work to leave on Thursday afternoon instead. I rebooked the tickets and sent him a playful text telling him I didn't think I could make it Friday after all. He asked, "Why?" and I texted back, "I met this guy and can't stop thinking about him."

With the text, I sent him a picture of my connecting gate at LAX to Honolulu. He called me immediately.

"Oh my God. Are you seriously coming right now? This is the best present ever."

Just the knowledge that I was flying in earlier lifted his mood. It made my day to make his day better and support him. I was glad that I could surprise him and get into Hawaii a day early.

We greeted each other at the gate, and he said our running joke: "I'm gonna hug you so hard people are gonna think I'm murdering you." He always liked to give me bear hugs where he tried to make the people around us think he was trying to murder me—murder by hugs.

We arrived at the hotel and shifted into a relaxed mood. I was tired from traveling, so we went up to the Signature Room to grab a bite to eat. I could tell that he just wanted to be with me and that my presence relieved whatever depression he was going through. Aside from our normal hand-holding, hugging, and rubbing legs, we weren't much for PDA, but this time he grabbed my face and pulled me in for the most tender kiss. It felt like a silent declaration from him that all was right in the world.

I had a telehealth therapy session while he was at work the next day. I was dealing with conflicted feelings that I couldn't seem to sort out. I was beginning to psych myself out. Things had felt a bit different since his trip to Detroit when he disappeared on me for a day. When that didn't quite turn out to be the alarm that I was on the lookout for, I thought I would feel better, but I still didn't. There was still this heaviness looming over me that I couldn't quite place. *Were our difficulties real or make-believe? Was I creating a situation in my mind that had not completely taken place in reality?* I didn't want to cause the derailment of something that could turn out well for me.

"I don't know what I'm doing," I told my therapist. "I feel like I am lying in wait for the other shoe to drop."

"Why do you think you feel that way?"

"Well, there's always something that ends up happening and this time feels no different. It's just the story of my life."

She helped me explore why I was thinking so glumly. I realized that it was because I wasn't sure where this relationship was going. We were having fun, but I wanted reassurance that I wasn't being taken for granted again. I had seen relationship after relationship fail, from childhood to my own adult years, and I always felt like I would not be exempt from that pattern.

Dale and I always enjoyed each other's company, and despite all the difficult conversations, we still seemed to be progressing, but there was still a weight to everything that I couldn't quite pinpoint. Our relationship was light, but the air wasn't. I grappled with needing to know and learn more. Something was amiss, and I didn't know if he felt this relationship was just for the meantime or not. I needed more—more comfort, more certainty. We had both said we loved each other, but what did that mean for the long term? Perhaps it was self-sabotage in a sense, but what if it was my gut speaking to me? I just didn't understand what I was trying to tell myself.

I texted Dale and let him know that I needed to share some things with him. When he returned to the hotel room, he seemed pensive and unsure. When he entered our room, his walk was uncertain, like he was in trouble but anxious to hear what he did wrong and ready to rectify it. He lay down next to me and said, "Okay, I'm ready."

I gave myself a few seconds to gather my thoughts, and then I said, "Babe, I know I've been a little off lately. I've been processing some things and I'm sorry if I made you feel like you did something wrong. I care about you, and this relationship means a lot to me, but I want to be intentional and make sure we're on the same page. How do you feel about us now? Where do you see us in the future?"

Dale sat up, seeming more relaxed and comfortable than when he initially sat down next to me, and responded with a big smile. "If we're still progressing like we are now—and I don't see much changing—you're gonna find yourself married again!"

"Really?"

"Absolutely!" he said, more loudly and with a bigger smile.

I asked him a few more questions about our future, and he responded calmly and straight to the point each time. The weight of insecurity that I had been carrying lifted, and I exploded in tears.

Now I was no longer on the ledge looking over into bleakness. I settled on the reality that I had just been self-sabotaging. I wasn't perfect at being self-aware, and I needed confirmation to continue to move forward with confidence. As much as I believed in love and knew it was out there for me, I still was afraid to put myself out there. I couldn't walk into another situation that would traumatize me. My previous relationship was so detrimental to my self-esteem and overall mental health that I just didn't have it in me to do it all over again. That relationship haunted me, and I had more work to do. But this was not a burden that Dale needed to bear.

I hadn't really been appropriately loved. I'd been used throughout my life, settling for another's warped version of what love was. I was tired of the drama and trauma. Seeing myself as a crutch or as somebody lacking in the most basic of areas, even after all the work I have done on and for myself, was humbling. I'd been the light that people were attracted to, while all they brought was darkness. Now that I recognized this about myself, I had to be even more intentional about who I allowed to be close to me.

Dale grabbed my face. "I'm so sorry. He really hurt you, didn't he?"

I nodded through my tears.

"Thank you for talking to me about things like this. One of the things I love about you is how perceptive and transparent you are. It helps me to be myself when I am around you. You're always so vulnerable." He gently wiped my tears away, kissing my wet face. "Isn't it scary to be like that all the time?"

"No, it's scarier when other people aren't vulnerable, and they take advantage of the fact that you have an open heart. I'm proud of myself. I haven't allowed the world and the broken people to kill my spirit."

He held me tightly. "I promise that I'm never going to hurt you."

We sat in the stillness of my truth for several moments, but Dale wouldn't be true to himself if he lingered there too long. He smiled and said, "Babe, the street isn't on fire!"

It was a reference to a story he had told me about a time he was on the job in Michigan detailing the vice president. They'd always plan for emergency routes and make contingency plans, and on this particular day, everything went to shit. They were working with State Patrol and learned that a street was actually on fire as part of their driving route. So whenever things were in full chaos, he'd always say that the street was on fire.

Before long, we were discussing our plans for the rest of our time in Hawaii. I wanted to do something different from our normal routines. There was more to the island than just Starbucks, the Signature Room, and karaoke.

Dale talked me into seeing that god-awful movie, *Cocaine Bear*. I had the idea of going to a strip club, because I enjoyed watching the talented women dance and the energy in the club. I was sexually aware and loved the sensuality of it. We had a good time and visited more than once. I even bought him a few dances.

We also hiked Diamond Head trail. Diamond Head was hard yet beautiful. Most say you focus more on the crater, but I was mesmerized by the vast blue sea and couldn't take my eyes off it. I tended to zone out in nature when hiking, but not this time. Dale was not much of a hiker but did it to get outside his comfort zone.

Dale claimed he once bowled a 300 in Martha's Vineyard, so we took it to the bowling lanes. We had been competitively jesting through the entire game. He bowled like a psycho—I thought he was going to bust a hole in the wall from the way he contorted his body to roll that ball. It was like a Tasmanian devil and the Road Runner had a baby who bowled. Despite his crazy bowling style, we had a great time at Lucky Strike. I was anxiously waiting for this talented bowler to show up as promised, but he never did, and I won all three games. Dale had no interest in a rematch.

When we finished our game, we watched the Super Bowl with his coworkers. Afterward, walking back to the hotel, he asked if he could show me something. It was a meme of a woman in a yoga pose with a quote that said, "Stop disturbing women you're not ready for."

"Do you believe that?" I asked.

"Yeah. You know, I need to work on a lot of things."

This affirmed my hope that we were going toward creating something healthy for ourselves. If we continued on this trajectory, we would be a power couple.

We prepared for another evening out, dressed in Hawaiian cute clothes for Valentine's Day. I felt confident in how far we had come as a couple and ready to celebrate the evening with my significant other. We decided to go to the restaurant on the water we had seen while swimming with the turtles. Unfortunately, we couldn't get a reservation, but there was room at the bar.

The restaurant was perfectly decorated, a chic, glass-walled dining room with a large terrace and stunning views overlooking Waikiki and Diamond Head. It looked like a set from a romantic movie. I was in the mood for something hearty, and as I reviewed the menu, I found nothing to satisfy my hunger. The restaurant was a fancy small-plate-style venue with a pre-fixed menu of beet risotto and other light delicacies.

We looked at each other, and without saying a word, we smiled and knew that we both wanted to go to another, smaller restaurant with comfort food and a more upbeat and youthful atmosphere. The new restaurant had a cheesy little Valentine's Day selfie station and loud island music playing overhead. It was perfect. We ate delicious wings and fries—so much more what we were in the mood for than the beet risotto. We took a few photos with the restaurant in the background and others as the night wore on. My flight was leaving the next day, so we headed back to our room relatively early so that I could relax and prepare for my departure.

C3

I had a favorite eatery at Honolulu International Airport that sold the best fish tacos. In anticipation of eating those before I boarded the plane, I had only a cup of coffee and a yogurt parfait for breakfast and skipped lunch. Dale came back from work to see me off and spend a little more time with me before I headed home.

As we were leaving for the airport, I got a notification that my flight would be delayed. I had an early work call the next day that I had to prepare for and couldn't miss. Meanwhile, my flight kept getting pushed back. Nervous that I might end up missing my call completely, I decided to rebook my flight for the afternoon the next day and just do the call from the hotel first.

We decided to sit out on the balcony while I worked on my reports. I wanted everything prepped and ready for the next day. After ten minutes, Dale said he was going to run to Target to get a few things. The hotel was connected by a parking lot next to the Ala Moana mall, which included Target, so it would be quick. I was engrossed in my work tasks. Before he left, he asked if I needed anything.

"Need anything while I'm out?"

"Mm, I'm pretty hungry."

"I'll be back soon, and we can go grab something to eat."

"Sounds good!" It wouldn't take long to finish my work, and then we could do whatever we wanted for the rest of the evening.

Thirty minutes later, which was an hour past starving, I saw him making his way back. He stood at the ramp eagerly waving at me to get my attention.

I finished up and was ready to eat, but Dale had still not appeared. I called him to find out that he was still running his mouth downstairs in the lobby. He knew I was starving before he left. At this point, I hadn't eaten anything all day. I was hangry waiting for him, and he was in the lobby gabbing with tourists.

"Sorry, Coco! I'm on my way."

Another twenty minutes passed. I was ready to stab somebody if I didn't start chewing and swallowing immediately. My stomach felt like it was eating itself, so I gave him another call. The ringing of the phone with no answer put me directly into bitch mode. I grabbed my things and left to get myself something to eat without him. As I left the hotel, I called him again. No answer. I started walking, hoping to find a restaurant that was open and looked decent. He finally returned my call while I walked in a daze.

"Where *are* you?" he asked.

I couldn't keep my composure. "What is *wrong* with you? I told you that I was hangry twenty minutes ago. You've been gone for an hour and a half!" I screamed into the phone as I walked down a busy street in Honolulu, a few minutes from Waikiki, surrounded by pedestrians, tourists, honking motorists, tons of honking, and homeless people.

"Why are you yelling at me?" He sounded genuinely shocked.

"Because you are so selfish!" I noticed the people around me staring.

"Where are you going?" he asked.

"Don't worry about it." I hung up. I didn't want to be around him. The only thing that was important to me was finding sustenance for my empty belly.

I found a restaurant and ordered a quick poké bowl. After I had demolished it, I began to feel more like myself. Once I did, I texted Dale to tell him I was wrong for yelling at him. I apologized for my outburst and told him I was disappointed that he had let so much time go by, even after my repeated requests. I couldn't think straight when running on fumes. I also told him that being hungry was not an excuse for my rudeness, but I felt he could be more considerate. It felt like one of his selfish moments.

I told him where I was and ordered some more food. When he arrived a little while later, I watched him walk around the bar looking for me. I was still annoyed, so I didn't call out to him. He stood right behind me, close enough to where I could feel his body heat. Then he texted me to turn around. *Why the hell does he make me smile when I want to frown and be upset?* He sat down on the stool next to me like a scolded child. For several seconds, we sat in complete silence.

"Is the food any good?" he asked, breaking the silence.

"Yeah." I grabbed his shoulder and growled. I wanted to shake him. I didn't want to blush—I wanted to be angry with him. His selfishness was frustrating, but it was so hard to stay mad at him.

# CATHARSIS

Dale told me about one of his co-workers doing some messy things with a girl. I had met this co-worker several times throughout our relationship, and every time, he was with a new girl. The last girl that I saw him with was... interesting. She had a thick East Coast accent and smoked two packs of Camel Lights a day. The girl felt there was something off in their relationship, so she messaged his ex on Instagram to confirm. While Dale couldn't believe the girl behaved that way, I couldn't believe his co-worker.

"There's no way a woman would do that unless the man tells her things that aren't adding up. There must be a legitimate reason she did that. Besides, she was trailer trash in the first place," I said.

I was dealing with some distressing challenges at work, so this conversation felt like just a bother. My boss was harassing me, making comments about how he'd "toss me around the bedroom," and remarking that he was a staunch Republican but proud of himself for hiring "someone like me." He was fired after an extensive investigation that found he was harassing several of his women direct reports. I hoped things might get better after he was fired, but retaliation came down hard from my VP who had been friends with my boss and blamed us for his termination. The topic of Dale's coworker's girlfriend felt like a waste of my time. I wanted to talk to Dale about something that mattered to me.

Dale was aware I was being harassed at work, but at no point in time had he inquired more, nor had I the opportunity to go into detail about what was going on. He would say, "How did your meetings wrap up?" and I would say something like, "I'm so exhausted from corporate America." He would say, "You're strong! I know you got this," and then change the subject.

I noticed that I was attentive to his moods and shifts, but he wasn't tuned in to mine. I was having a rough time emotionally, and I wanted to be able to communicate with him, receive support, and be the focus to relieve my stresses and worries for a change.

I gave up on trying to get him to discuss my frustrations further and felt like it was best that we finish our conversation and try another time. Right as our conversation was ending, another friend of his called. We said our goodbyes, he switched to his other call, and I sat alone with my thoughts.

Later that evening, I called again, but he said that he was on the phone with his son, so I requested that he call me when he was done. An hour later, I texted to see if he was still on the phone. He said he was. I found it suspicious given his communication patterns with his son, but I let it go. Another hour rolled by, and still no callback. I called him, upset.

I left him a voicemail: "I know you're not still on the phone with your son. Please don't lie to me."

He was adamant that he was still talking with his son. This angered me further because in all the time I had known him, his calls with his teenage son had typically been five- to ten-minute calls. Dale texted me back and assured me he was on the phone with his son and would call me as soon as he got off. Time still ticked on, but there was no return call.

I was hot, and I texted him: "You are on some bullshit. I know you aren't talking to your son." I wasn't interested in playing games with him. It didn't matter who he was talking to. The problem was that he was playing with my emotions because he clearly knew I was in a mood, which was probably the real reason he wasn't returning my call. I demanded that he be a man and just say he didn't want to speak to me until I calmed down.

When he finally admitted that he was talking to another friend, I was pissed. I felt like I was always there for him, but the moment I was in need, I was left hanging to sort things out by myself. I was struggling with getting work emails and text messages after hours, and having major panic attacks every night as I tried to prepare for the next working day. I would have one day a week, Saturday, that I felt okay and then by Sunday evening, the onset of anxiety would kick in at the thought of another work week—the "Sunday scaries." We had spent months dealing with his internal conflicts. It was okay for me to do cartwheels for him, but for me, nothing.

He picked up on my mood and decided to avoid me altogether. It was starting to sink in for me that his selfishness may be a significant obstacle in our relationship. His support was what I needed most of all, and I was beginning to think I would never receive it. I sent him a text: "Stop playing with my fucking emotions!" Then I called him and lost it, cussing him out and going off.

"Are you ready to be calmer?" he asked.

"No," I said.

"I'm sending you an email now, and I need you to read it. I can't talk to you tonight. We can talk tomorrow about what I'm going to tell you. I planned to speak to you, but I'm in a bad state right now, and the conversation wouldn't go well. My email is going to be a little long but wait for it please."

My desire was for him to be a man and have a difficult conversation. He wasn't showing up for me. I hung up the phone.

I waited for the email, talking with a friend on the phone to defragment my emotions, and told her how he had escalated my temper.

By midnight, I still had not received anything. It was tough for me to sleep that night because I was still angry. I tossed and turned all night long. I checked my phone every thirty minutes or so. I turned on a few shows that would distract me from checking my phone incessantly. I finally received the email at four in the morning.

*Coco,*

*You once asked me to tell you something I haven't told anyone else about myself. I once told you that my ex called me stupid because I did something she didn't like. The night she did that, I blacked out. I remember everything going dark, and I felt like I was standing beside myself, watching myself, about to do something horrible. The only thing that snapped me out of it was that my son started crying because of all the yelling. I told you about grabbing my keys and driving downtown to get some drinks to calm down.*

*When you called me earlier, I was on the phone speaking to my son, and you immediately raised your voice at me when I said I would call you back. It instantly put me on defense. I don't do confrontation well in relationships when I feel as though someone is being overly aggressive.*

*I have a problem with how a person speaks to me, not what they say. I think one prime example with you is when I misinterpreted how you were speaking to me in Hawaii at RumFire that one evening when you told me to "shut the fuck up" in an elevated voice. I couldn't bring myself to call you back last night because I felt the conversation would escalate to a level that I would have a problem dealing with.*

*The truth is, I do a great job of showing happiness on the outside. Internally, I go through swings of sadness, depression, loneliness, anger, and some other stuff that I can't put into words. In a nutshell, I'm not in the right mindset to make you happy consistently, even though you have told me I make you happy. I've got issues I've got to work through, and I apologize to you for dragging you into something you didn't ask for. Last night, you said I was playing with your emotions, and that really hit me hard because I take emotions seriously, mainly because I run through so many of them at any given time. I've always hated the line, "It's not you, it's me," but nothing could be more accurate in this case.*

90

*I want to speak to you to answer any questions you may have, but after this honest emotional release, I will have to gather myself a bit. To quote the late great Tupac, "This is the realist shit I ever wrote." That is a complete fact.*

*Dale*

It was a heavy email. How did last night somehow go full circle and back to him again? I was the one in need of support that he wouldn't give. Once again, I found myself trying to run to his rescue and help him through another crisis.

I called a friend, and she asked if I wanted to deal with this. It was a lot to take on when I already had a household of kids who needed my support, attention, and guidance. I started to feel hopeless about the potential for a healthy and long-lasting relationship. I was a fixer and my heart was all in, so I always jumped to help others without receiving the same support when the tables were turned. I had already invested much time, money, and energy with him. To start all over and maybe not find someone as open as he was to change would be a loss. Maybe I was living the sunk cost fallacy, but it felt real.

I responded to his email by telling him that I loved him and supported him. I spent the rest of the day going through the motions. I got my kids on the bus for school and pushed through the work day. I sat on call after call for work, but my mind was always going back to him. I needed more time to process his email before we discussed it further. The more I talked to my friends about it, the more they were worried that he had too many issues and that I shouldn't try to handle them.

I hoped and expected that the people closest to me would desire the best for me. He and I were talking about commitment and a future marriage, so I was all in—just for the rug to be pulled from underneath me.

After the email, our conversations seemed to focus back on his fears and anxieties again. Dale was consistently emotional. Every phone call had its heavy moments, and he broke down in tears every time we talked. It felt like he needed support and was unraveling.

He didn't know what was wrong with him.

I told him I thought he was going through catharsis. All his repressed emotions were being released, and with that came intense feelings and reactions. His walls were crumbling around him.

Dale began to recall childhood memories, admitting that he could count on one hand how many times he had said "I love you" to his father. He told me that one time, as a seven-year-old kid, he ran to hug and kiss his dad, but his father stopped him and said, "Men don't kiss men." Dale would begin to cry uncontrollably and then say he wasn't able to talk right then and would call me later, a pattern that was becoming alarming.

I made sure I stayed aware of the things we were talking about because I knew that it was emotionally exhausting for him. Once you got to that place, you just shed all the shit so that you could metamorphose into the person you wanted to become. The process was draining, though. He would call me later, feeling more refreshed, but would say he felt like his vulnerability had made him soft. He had a false perception of what manhood was and did not seem to understand that there was strength in vulnerability.

I wanted him to get to the beauty of loving who he was and working on himself so that he could love his authentic self. I wanted him to live a life of purpose as I did so that we could continue to walk the path into the future together.

# ASPEN PLEASE

With Dale in crisis mode, my autopilot kicked in; I immediately entered a "fix my baby" mindset. I'd talked with my therapist about the experience of being parentified—as the oldest of four children, I had been in charge a lot at a young age, from making meals to putting on Band-Aids and solving conflicts. I never knew what a boundary was. I allowed others to push limits without repercussions because nobody had taught me how to do anything else. I was a pleaser.

With Dale, this showed up as being the fixer. I struggled watching him self-destruct trying to navigate his own life's struggles. I worried it was impossible and wanted to help him. I was in a "we" frame of mind, and it felt like he still wasn't ready. He said he afraid the floodgates would open, and he would no longer be able to keep them closed or protect himself. He was scared to be vulnerable or in his mind, "soft." He would often tell me that I was bringing out Soft Dale and he didn't like it, so he'd do or say something to make himself feel tough again.

My goal was to show him that I would be there for him in the good and the bad, and maybe, through time, he could learn to do the same for me.

I proposed that he go to therapy so that he could continue the process with professional help. He had a lot to unpack, and although he felt safe sharing with me, I thought it was too much to put on me. I told him that I was his person and would continue to support him, but he needed more resources than I could give alone.

He seemed open to the idea and decided that he would give it a try. Within a day, I created and sent him a list of fifteen Black male therapists who offered in-office sessions. All he had to do was choose one and schedule an appointment.

I had his back and would not abandon him when things weren't going well. That's what couples are supposed to do for each other; they should hold it down when the other needs support, right? I continued to talk about our relationship in my own therapy sessions. My goal was for him to see for himself what he needed and then create his own plan of attack.

That week, Dale was working overnights. I worked all day, cared for the kids, and then after their bedtime I stayed up on the phone with him all night. I was barely getting any sleep.

He desperately wanted me to come to Aspen, and I wanted to be there for him so we could weather this storm together.

I spoke with my mother about some of the struggles we were having and asked her if she would be free to be with the kids for a few days. My mother eagerly accepted time with her grandbabies. Even looking back and seeing some of the ways my childhood set me up to struggle with relationships, I gave her grace for who she was and knew what she went through with my dad and her own childhood experiences. Our relationship had gotten to a solid place, and she was an amazing grandma.

I ran my availability by Dale for when we could get together for a long weekend while he was in Aspen. "If I'm coming to Aspen, you know you're getting outside of your comfort zone, right?"

Dale wasn't much of an outdoor person, especially when it came to winter activities. The thought of snowboarding, skiing, or snowmobiling never crossed his mind.

"I know..." He took a deep breath. "What are we doing?"

"We're going to go snowmobiling, ice skating, and skiing or snowboarding. We're going to do white people shit!"

He was game. When I pulled up at the condo, he was outside waiting for me and gave me the usual bear hug, but it felt hollow— sad and heavy. He seemed like a shell of himself.

My mission felt clear: I would help him fill himself up again. Despite some challenges recently, I hoped he would offer me the same support when I found myself in difficult times in the future, and I set aside the recent issues and shortcomings. He gave me a tour of the ski condo, displaying the hospitality he was known for, though his usual zeal seemed muted and tired. There were spurts of his chipper self, such as when he was excited to show me that he'd already purchased a few grocery items for me: grape tomatoes, avocadoes, lettuce, and rosé. The extra hugs and kisses I gave were comforting to him. I could tell because he leaned into them like a child.

We decided to go for breakfast right away because we were both famished. Dale found this cute little restaurant in town. He had heard they had the best corned beef hash, with which he was obsessed.

"Babe, I don't think it's gonna be good here," I said as we sat down, shaking my head.

The waitress told us that it was canned and not fresh, but Dale ordered the corn beef hash anyway. After the first taste, he agreed that it was trash. Everything was mushed and it looked like a toddler prepared a meal of dog food.

After our mediocre breakfast, we walked around town to do a little shopping. We piddled around a few stores in town looking for snow gear for him.

We didn't waste too much time shopping because he worked overnights and wanted to get some rest before his shift. We returned to the condo to rest and book our excursions for the next few afternoons so he could sleep directly after work. For one afternoon, we booked skiing and on another a snowmobile trip. Dale was the most excited about our snowmobile outing. I wanted things to go smoothly, and I didn't want him to worry much in his already moody state.

We quickly fell into our routine. That first day, we just explored, walked around, and greeted every other person of color we happened to see. We were crossing the street and saw another Black couple. I yelled "Hey, Black people!" and the girl and I embraced each other. She was wearing the knee-high faux fur boots that I kept seeing around town. We talked about their comfort and style, and the guys quickly chatted it up about where they were from and what activities they had been doing.

The next day, I saw Dale was interested in trying something new but was nervous about it. He bought us tickets to take the gondola so I could see the full view of the mountains. It was terrific, although a blizzard meant most of the view was blurred by snow. I took some pictures in the gondola, and we took pictures with a quirky group of guys with Nicki Minaj flags.

The more time we spent together, the more I could feel him releasing all the pent-up negative energy he felt. It was like watching ice slowly melt. It felt good to know my presence was a calming force in his life; I was happy to be around him and to be there to help him. After wine and a good conversation, we returned to our room. We relaxed before dinner, and before he had to get to work, I brought up the email.

"I wanted to ask you in person so I could see your eyes. You said something in your email about how you saw yourself doing something bad. You saw yourself doing something to your ex-wife?"

"Yeah," he said.

"You didn't, right?" I just was hoping he hadn't put his hands on her.

"No, I didn't."

"So, you didn't hit her, right?"

"No, we talked about that. I left the house instead."

I remembered that, and I could relax with confirmation from him.

We sat on the couch watching *CNN* while he rubbed my feet. He asked more questions about what to expect with therapy and therapists before *CNN* began to disrupt our calm.

"*CNN* irks my soul now," I remarked.

"What do you mean?"

"I'm not a fan of *CNN* because they're so biased."

We went back and forth about what shows we watched faithfully and why. Normalcy began to return to his voice and posture. Our previous awkward conversations only felt like life hurdles that we had overcome together as a couple. I asked him what he needed.

"My mind takes on so many different emotions and thoughts at the same time. I feel like nobody truly understands who I am except for you. I don't know."

I had again talked to my therapist about us, and she had told me to ask more questions to get a better grasp of his traumas. I also needed to be clear about my boundaries.

"What do we need to be doing more or less of in our relationship to get to where we need to be?" I asked him.

"More talks. More communication where I feel like I can shed my past." He thought deeper on the question and added, "I think we do a really good job of traveling, date nights, and hanging out. I love our talks the most."

"Me too!"

We were still snuggled on the couch, not worried about the world.

"And more of this. Just sitting, relaxing, just the two of us." Dale smiled. I liked hearing this explicitly from him.

☙

The next day, we woke up early to go snowmobiling. I felt rewarded by getting people to have fun outside of their comfort zone. I liked how, at first, he was nervous about our planned activities. He couldn't believe I had him out there snowmobiling. Once he got going, though, he put the pedal to the metal. He drove, allowing me to take in all the scenery. The snow-covered trees against the sky as a backdrop were beautifully romantic and eye-catching. The cold air against my cheeks, in contrast to the warmth of my coat with my arms around my guy, put me in a good mood. We met some friendly people during our ride and had a blast. It was an incredible experience. He had never driven a snowmobile, but he loved it.

There were a bunch of sisters from down south on our drive with their cute southern accents. We overheard one of them discussing her son moving to Detroit with disdain. She was asking, "Who would *want* to move to Detroit?" We let her know that we were both from "The D"—a "watch what you say" kind of thing. Detroit is so much more than what's portrayed on the news. There's an energy, a grit, a culture, a pride like nowhere else.

We continued snowmobiling, and one of the sisters was not paying attention and took this curve that blew her and her tiny sister off the snowmobile into a ditch. The guides had to help them out of the snow. The snow had continued to drift, so the guides had to leave the snowmobile there, which we laughed about. It felt like payback for her earlier comments.

Halfway through our tour, we got off the snowmobiles and went inside this cute little hut for hot beverages to warm us up. I got hot cider, and Dale got hot cocoa. We stood in the corner enjoying our drinks and warming up. He asked if I wanted to drive the snowmobile for the next half, which was the speed circuit, and I told him no.

A couple from the tour started chatting us up. They were also a long-distance couple and dated for two years before one moved to California to be together. The woman asked us, "So, who's moving? Virginia or Minnesota?"

I got a bit uncomfortable and immediately said, "Cart before the horse... We'll figure that out at the appropriate time."

A bunch of guys from Saudi Arabia also pulled up to the hut from a different tour. Dale struck up a conversation with them because he'd traveled to Saudi Arabia before. They began to discuss the sights, the culture, and a well-known restaurant that he enjoyed, which one of the guys happened to own. During their conversation, they told Dale he should go skiing. They had gone skiing the day before for the first time ever, loved it, and encouraged him to take the bull by the horns. It was already our plan, but he hadn't been as excited about skiing as snowmobiling.

To help the process, I found some ski places where he could rent the equipment, as I was already prepared with my snow gear, goggles, and snowboard. We went first thing the following morning after he got off work. We were making the most of our time together, with him getting the bare minimum amount of sleep. After renting out his ski equipment, I strongly recommended that he take a lesson.

I knew I couldn't teach him. He reminded me of the time he learned to swim by jumping in and going for it, even though he almost drowned. Everyone tried to convince him, from the associates at the ski rental place to the other guests on our snowmobiling tour.

"Dale, you'll benefit from an instructor, they can teach you the basics and you'll get more out of your time," I said.

Dale was so stubborn. I knew he would hurt himself, but he wanted to do it himself, so I let it go. I showed him the basics, pizza and french fry, but an instructor would benefit him more. After a few basic skills at the base, we hopped on the chairlift to go up the bunny hill, and I tried to explain to him how to get off the lift while heading to the top.

"Since you have skis, basically just stand up and slide down. Watch the penguin. Keep your eyes on the penguin right there. Stand up and push off but hold your ski sticks," I said.

"Okay, okay," he kept saying the whole way up with little confidence.

The closer we got to the top, the more he began to panic. On the way up the gondola, I was taking pictures of us and telling him to smile.

He muttered, "Oh my God, I can't believe I'm doing this shit. I'm comfortable in this chair but it's moving so slowly. Oh my God. Penguin! Oh my God."

He was riling himself up with nervous energy, and I knew this would not turn out well. I couldn't calm him or get him to repeat what I said correctly. We were both on edge by the time we reached the top.

The attendants had to stop the chairlift at the top because Dale busted his ass getting off and took me down with him. We both ate snow trying to get off. I was embarrassed. He had the most challenging time getting his skis on, and when he finally got them on, he leaned back and fell again. We were on the bunny hill. I had known his first run wouldn't go smoothly, but I hadn't expected it would take him forty-five minutes to get down one run because he couldn't figure out how to step into his bindings.

Meanwhile, I sat there, strapped into my snowboard, waiting. I would make a little loop now and again, but mostly, I just sat and watched him. It looked pathetic, and I was in tears from laughter, but when he looked my way, I held it in. He was dripping sweat as if he had run for forty-five minutes. I wanted to do more than just the bunny hill. I thought about going down an actual mountain, and as I looked back in Dale's direction, I saw him collide with the helper managing the lift. She was trying to pick random people to give him lessons, and now they were both eating snow. This big, grown-ass man wobbling around while kids were zooming by was funny. After two hours, though, his stubbornness began to put a damper on my enjoyment.

So I finally thought, *Fuck this.* I got up and said, "Babe, I'm gonna do a few runs by myself and head to the restaurant."

He agreed and apologized. I checked on him a few times as I was passing him by on the run and he was continuing to struggle.

I was done for the day. Needing a boost, I decided to grab lunch to rejuvenate my energy. Unable to bear watching him clumsily navigate any longer, I opted for wings and a drink at the bar, where I chatted with a few local patrons. He finally came to join me half an hour later, dripping in sweat.

"I hurt myself," he said when he arrived at the bar. "I'm going to rest for a little bit and then go back out."

After removing his gear, he ordered food and pulled out his phone. I saw another text from Tisha: "I hope you have a fantastic day!"

This did not help my irritation at all. Here I was, trying to calm down, and this bitch was texting. I thought I had clearly addressed my concerns about her the first time. I was no longer in the mood for anything. I was ready to head back to the condo and do anything but deal with this situation.

We ate, and I focused on my food without talking much. After we finished our meals and settled the bill, he decided he was done skiing for the day. This was a relief, because I was certain he'd end up breaking his neck.

We made our way back to the condo to shower and squeeze in a quick nap before dinner. The plan was to go to dinner around six so he could be at work by nine. I had enough time to regulate my emotions, so instead of napping, I addressed the elephant on my side of the room.

"I saw the message from Tisha." I went straight to the point, no sugarcoating. "Why is she still sending you these random text messages?"

He pulled out his phone. "I didn't even see that."

"I saw it."

"I told you I don't respond to her."

"Okay, I don't know if you're being dismissive or not, but I'm gonna ask you this right now. Did you check Tisha the first time I told you? I realized we weren't together then and we made it official after that conversation, but did you check her? Did you talk to her about it?"

"Well, I mean, no, because she doesn't really reach out to me."

His nonchalant attitude was confusing, especially when he definitely knew how I felt about her texting. It didn't matter if he thought I was overreacting; it mattered because I had expressed my concerns. It seemed as if he didn't care about my feelings. My chest tightened, suffocating under the weight of unspoken frustrations. I clenched my fists, nails digging into my palms as I fought to contain the rising tide of indignation. But like a dam strained beyond capacity, my restraint crumbled. Sharp and heated words burst forth like a sudden geyser, propelled by the force of pent-up emotion.

"I don't give a fuck! I find it disrespectful if she knows that you have a woman and she's still texting messages like that. As a woman, I would never reach out to anybody else's man like that. I don't even reach out to my homeboys like that."

"I don't understand why you're freaking out about this. I barely talk to her. She just sends me random ass text messages every now and then." He shrugged and shook his head as if it was no big thing.

"At the end of the day, you don't have to understand what I feel or what I deem to be disrespectful. It's important for you to listen to me, and if I'm telling you that those actions feel off to me as a woman, then you need to respect that." My blood was boiling. "If I have guy friends that are doing something that is even remotely close to being disrespectful to you in our relationship, I'm checking that shit. I'm going to nip it in the bud right then and there. The fact that I told you I found that disrespectful and you didn't address it with her is concerning." I took a breath. "I will not allow this relationship to turn me into an insecure or jealous person. That's not who I want to be. And this is a problem for me. I already told you this a couple of months ago. I'm not about checking phones. I'm not about checking emails, iPads, shit like that. But if I ever feel like I have to start being in that position, I'm out." I hoped I was more straightforward with my feelings and what he needed to do to correct the problem.

"Fine," he conceded, but then tried to explain. "You just don't get her. She's just like a quintessential Southern girl."

"Dale, I don't care where she's from. I'm telling you, I find her actions disrespectful. As a grown-ass woman, if she's forty-five years old, she should know better. The fact that I've already talked to you about this and you didn't address it with her shows me you don't really care or understand what the issue is."

"Fine," he said dismissively. "I'll call her and talk to her."

"What are you going to say?" His attitude irked my soul.

"I'm gonna tell her that my girlfriend doesn't appreciate it."

"All you have to do is, as a man, be like, 'Listen, you know that I'm in a relationship. You need to fall back.'"

It pissed me off that he didn't have a problem with it. His concern was more about me having an issue with her texts. I no longer felt like napping. I went outside on the patio to sit and collect my thoughts and emotions. I called my friend to talk, and she tried to shift my energy before returning inside. Here I was on this trip, trying to lift his spirits, and he was negating mine again. I had to consciously stop glancing at his phone—I was not about to turn into a worrier who walked up behind their partner to see what they were doing.

I could see him shifting like he had in San Francisco. The instability made me uneasy. We had only one or two days left, and I needed to forcibly change the energy to get back on track to loving each other.

Over dinner, I began by telling him that I loved him and was not interested in fighting with him. "I can't expect you to move through this world like me. But I do expect you to take my thoughts and concerns into consideration. I'm disappointed that you didn't address it the first time, and now we have to have this conversation again. I'm dropping this conversation now. The ball's in your court. I'm not looking at your phone anymore. But I hope you address this situation."

After that, he told me that he had finally managed the situation. I put my feelings of alarm to rest so I could move forward with hope instead of concern.

Before he went to work, he listed a few spots he had been to and knew the bartenders would take care of me. Dale made sure I had an assigned bike person who would take me to places around town, so I didn't have to walk home at night by myself. His adjustment allowed me to let it go, and I wiped the slate clean, holding no grudges. I wanted to continue to be sympathetic toward him, as I hoped he would be to me in return.

Dale attempted to make biscuits, eggs, and bacon in the morning. I could sense some frustration with him waiting for the biscuits to be done.

"Did you adjust the recipe for baking at high altitude?"

He settled down immediately. We sat like this old couple just hanging out watching *CNN* and *Al Jazeera*. The rest of the time, we spent in the hot tub and having a lot of sex. Our physical connection was intense, and we couldn't keep our hands off each other.

I felt safe with him. He wasn't perfect, but I felt like he was trying, and I had to give him credit where credit was due. The rest of the weekend was lovely.

We both cried at the airport during my departure. He pulled up to the airport and grabbed my suitcase from the trunk. We were holding hands the entire way there. As he shut the door to the trunk, he grabbed me and held me close, and I started bawling.

"Babe, please stop, or I'm gonna start crying again," he said.

"I love you and hate leaving you, but we'll get through this."

He started crying.

A cute airport worker smiled at us and said, "Aw, look at this lovely goodbye." He looked like someone you'd want to hang out with. The distraction gave Dale time to pull himself together.

Dale and I smiled, shared one last hug and kiss, and I walked into the airport.

# DISSOCIATION

As I prepared for my journey back to Hawaii, I cradled the phone against my ear, multitasking as I packed my bag. "I'm so excited to see you again!"

I was consumed with my eagerness, but there was a sudden shift in our conversation to his frustrations. He told me that he had been reprimanded at work. I could sense his heaviness through the phone. It was a weird, unfamiliar energy.

"I don't even have a consistent schedule anymore. They're just throwing me on morning shift, then night shift, then midday. It's chaos," he complained.

I was initially supposed to join them in Australia, but they took him off the trip and sent him to Hawaii for another three weeks instead. Then a day or two before I was supposed to leave for Hawaii, he called me frantically annoyed because his time in Hawaii had been cut short. He told me the day before I was supposed to board the plane. Everything was up in the air. His boss informed him via email that his new assignment would start on Tuesday in Maryland, working as a professor training new agents.

He was no longer assigned to the Obama detail.

Dale felt his new boss was cracking down on the casual attire the agents wore around the Obamas. He had seen Dale wearing gym shoes at a restaurant and reprimanded everyone out of uniform. His boss had recently sent someone else home from a trip for wearing a hoodie.

"I'm going to email him," Dale said.

"What do you plan to say?" I asked, but he was getting even more pissed with every moment. He was using me to express his thoughts and process his rage. I felt like I could be unwavering support for him, so he at least was afforded an opportunity to get it all out before he sent his email. I was back in fix-it mode without being asked or given a moment's notice.

After he vented to me, he emailed his boss. His boss called him, and he found out that the changes were indeed because of the gym shoes. Dale, having seniority, was being made into an example for newer agents coming to the field. His boss, who was also Black, said, "Look, the Obamas have a predominantly Black team of agents, and we need to be just as professional as any other detail." He felt like the agents had relaxed their attire, and perhaps it was due to them being too comfortable and not diligent enough about the rules and expectations. He wanted them to step their game up and not be too relaxed.

Despite having my flight booked, I was unsure if I was actually heading to Hawaii. Dale told me to come anyway, and he would figure out the rest while I was in the air. He ended up being able to take some time off before he started his new assignment, so he didn't have a schedule at all while I was there. We had more flexibility to do whatever we wanted to do. He suggested that we start by grabbing a bite to eat at Duke's. I agreed and asked if we could go to the beach afterward to watch the sunset.

The night of my arrival, we saw this cute couple. The guy wore a cute pair of blue shorts with pink flamingos. I suggested he get some like the guy we saw with the pink flamingos because I thought they were masculine but sexy. Dale came back from Macy's with the exact pair that I mentioned, which made me happy.

He put on his pink flamingo blue shorts, and I put on my swimsuit and coverup. We made our way to Duke's. The streets were busy, and several streets were blocked off, which was a little frustrating. I was glad I wasn't driving.

"Are you okay?" Dale asked.

"I'm fine, babe. Are you good?" I threw the question back at him.

"Yeah. Just want to make sure you aren't stressed with the traffic." It was not the first time he had mentioned how easygoing I was in the car compared to his ex-wife.

After about half an hour in traffic, we arrived at Duke's. There were more Black people at the restaurant that day than we'd ever seen before. They were mainly from the East Coast and LA, with a few British folks sprinkled throughout the bar. Coincidentally, Dale knew one of the guys from a work trip to LA a few years back. It was some random association where they bonded, and we talked to them for hours. One of the couples ended up inviting us out that night.

Dale's phone rang, and he stepped out to take it. Later, he informed me that the call was about engraved watches that marked the conclusion of their tenure with the president, featuring the number 44. After giving them out to his team, the manager had one of the watches appraised and discovered that it was a thousand dollars over the value of what was allowed to be gifted to them, so he was calling all the agents to have them return the watches.

After Dale got off the call with his boss, he called other agents to talk about how ridiculous the manager was. Some had already sold or gifted their watches. I sat alone at the bar, feeling unattended. I finally signaled to him to get off the phone. He hung up, came over, and began to tell me the story. But I really didn't care; I was up in my feelings once again.

Maybe the universe was exposing the truth by taking off my rose-colored glasses. My demeanor was that I didn't give a fuck. I wanted to engage in conversations about real life instead of always being focused on his drama every time we were together. He was easily distracted and overlooked my needs at the drop of a hat. I always listened to his cries, but I was still dealing with some serious issues with discrimination at my job and still had not been given a chance to talk about it. I couldn't take another moment to hear his sob story about having to give back a watch. Not one moment of his time was spent checking on how I was feeling, but over a half hour was spent speaking with his friends about their engraved watches.

"I don't care!" I interrupted.

"Are you annoyed?"

"Yeah." I was irritated with him and needed some fresh air. "Let's just go outside."

I had already compromised so he could indulge in junk food from this bar. I had been putting on a smiling face, trying to enjoy myself and forget about my troubles, but lately, it felt like Dale was becoming more of a problem than a source of comfort. The bar was overcrowded, and I no longer wanted to be there. I wanted a change of scenery, some frozen drinks, and relaxation on the beach.

We found a place to lie on the beach.

He grabbed my hand. "Are you a bit calmer?"

"Yes, I'm trying to get there." I looked at him and was able to smile a little. "This is settling."

The sounds of the ocean waves washed away my negative mood and replaced it with warm fuzzy feelings. The sun descended, and the skies looked like an artist's palette. I no longer felt the negativity. I was reminded of my peace and how hard I fought to get to this space and place. I wasn't going to let anyone take it from me. I wasn't sure how or when the conversation between us picked back up, but it felt like old times when we enjoyed each other before all the selfish and immature moments disrupted our connection.

I began to think about his mental health, and if he had started on this journey already, knowing things could be a lot more promising for our relationship than if he hadn't. And if he hadn't, I needed to continue encouraging him to do so for us and himself. I wanted him to be better.

"Have you had a chance to call any of the therapists?"

"I reached out to some. I sent a couple of emails, but I haven't heard back."

"Sometimes people are just busy. Continue to be persistent."

Dale began scrolling through his phone, showing me the

profiles of people and other information he had gathered about each of them. "Okay, we will call them first thing Monday morning."

He changed the topic to some funny things he had seen online and began sharing them with me. There was another comfortable silence between us before I thought of his father.

"Have you spoken to your dad today?"

Dale began to talk about their recent conversation. He cried when he discussed his dad's mortality. His ability to be vulnerable comforted me because it validated that I was his person.

"I feel like I'm failing you," he said abruptly.

"Elaborate?"

"I've surrounded myself with people who have essentially placated my selfishness for so long. I've built these walls that I'm scared to break down. With you I'm breaking them down. How am I going to break them down and talk to a therapist?" I was unsure where this conversation was going, but I knew I could not continue to be his acting therapist. I wanted to be his woman, not his help, and I was a tech consultant, not a therapist.

Dale began telling me stories about him and his family, and the hardness of his upbringing. His family used humor as a tool, a defense mechanism. I recognized everything he described. I often pushed him to dig deep so I could see more than the clown he always presented to others. I pushed him to say more than the surface-level shit he liked to talk about.

"It's hard because I have all these negative people around me. My boy called me the other day and was bitching about his fiancée and her tiny ass dog. He told me, 'Sometimes I think I need to just be by myself.'"

He lost me when he abruptly shifted the conversation away from himself.

He pulled out his phone to show me yet another video on Instagram. This video was with Ace Metaphor. The topic was about "unready men" just trying to have a good time. Maybe they hook up a couple of times. They fall for that woman because she is the whole package, but they aren't ready to receive that package. Unready men string women along because they have gone through life unchecked and have not gone to therapy. An unready man will meet that one woman who changes their life, bringing out the spark, fire, and purpose that they've never had in their entire life. They are trying to get ready in the process but can't keep up. Because they are not prepared, they fuck it up. Then they fuck her up in the process because they haven't done the work.

"Ready men are equipped with the right things and don't need to string women along because they have a toolbox to problem-solve, compromise, and be in a healthy relationship," he said. "Ready men have done the work. They're in a place of maturity and self-acceptance. They're continuously working on ways to level up, so they are already prepared."

I was quiet. *That might apply to us, especially if we don't get him into therapy soon.*

"I don't want to lose you," he continued. "I have to get ready, and I hate that. I've got you in this situation like I'm stringing you along. You honestly caught me off guard. You hooked me. I have to drop my walls, but I'm in a place of discomfort."

*What did this man want me to say?* I was already in love with him. Maybe all the signs were the universe's way of revealing the red flags I had dismissed. When I saw them, I felt guilty and was unsure how to react. *How could I just throw him away when I knew I was his person?* I had told him I would be there for him and wouldn't drop him as soon as the going got tough, so what could I do with the signs now that I was so far in? I got lost in my inner thoughts about what he had just said.

I half-listened as Dale continued to talk, caught in the middle of a hyperventilated cry. He was talking about his mom. He wished that she was still here while recalling a story of how she never saw him graduate from the police academy many years ago. He hid his face from the other people on the beach.

"I haven't cried this much my entire life," he said. "I don't think I even cried this much at my mother's funeral." This was familiar, and of course, the analyst in me wanted to dig deeper.

"Where do you want to be in life?" I thought about the horrible relationship I had with my ex-boyfriend. When I had turned forty,

I committed myself to the second half of my life and to find my joy and happiness. I no longer wanted to deal with bullshit for the rest of my life. I settled with the fact that whether I ever actually obtained good, healthy love, I knew that I deserved it.

"I want to be happy, but I'm so afraid of being vulnerable," he said. "I've held this in for fifty-plus years... I feel safer when it's just me dealing with my shit and not being called out."

"Do you feel like you could ever get to a place of dropping your guard and opening up?"

He looked me in the eyes and said, "Incoming Soft Dale... you're the biggest treat a brother could hope for."

The sun started to set, and the beach staffers removed the beach chairs. He was calmer, and I was in a better head space. Instead of heading back to the hotel, Dale wanted to stay on the beach and continue talking, so we did. He shared more about his family life as a child and now as a father. I spoke of my childhood and my life as a single mother. We began to explore what our life would look like if we continued on this trajectory together and into the future. When and how would the first introductions be made? Why did it feel essential for me to wait to introduce men to my children?

We lay on the beach, watching the waves and talking while he played in the sand. He began to retell the story about when he killed the cat and problems in his marriage. While he was speaking, I thought about everything he was saying in his confessions. I did not feel fear at the red flags he retold. I was his safe space to express his feelings, and I continued to be a good listener.

"Remember when I told you that I saw myself doing something really bad to my ex?"

"Yeah."

"What did you think I was talking about?" His voice was weirdly calm.

"I assumed you were talking about hitting her." I looked at him, expecting a reply, but he said nothing and kept playing in the sand. "You didn't hit her, right?" I felt like I could handle emotional abuse dynamics and navigate them successfully, but physical abuse felt like it was somehow in a different category. I was thinking about triggers as I waited for him to respond.

"Yeah, no, I didn't hit her." Dale looked at me, flicking sand and lying comfortably on his side. "But I wasn't talking about hitting her."

*What the hell he was talking about then?* His answer unsettled me. I froze, confused, and didn't budge as I waited for him to finish. He sat silently, still staring at me, and I began to probe.

"Then what are you talking about?"

He looked at me with glossed-over eyes that looked vacant. "I was talking about killing her," he calmly stated.

I was in shock at hearing those words come out of his mouth so matter-of-factly. I didn't say anything. There were tons of people around, the waves were crashing, and all I could hear was his calm, eerie voice and nothing more. He looked so comfortable at that moment, and I was not. The way he continued to look at me commanded my attention in frozen silence. I didn't prompt him to continue; I couldn't speak. For once, I was at a loss for words.

"I was going to choke her," he continued. "I wanted to watch her take her very last breath."

I was aghast; my thoughts were empty, and my silence chained all words, even the ones that generally roamed inside my head. I felt paralyzed in a mix of freeze and fawn. I couldn't move, but I didn't want to create more conflict. I also wanted to fix the situation—fix him. But I couldn't do anything.

The feeling of freezing brought me back to when I saw my mom try to die as a child. One night, I heard her crying and went into her room. I yelled at her that she was being unfaithful to my dad who was trying to get home but was hiding away because of the war in Liberia. She swallowed a bunch of pills and said, "I'm sorry." I cried and pleaded, begging for her to stop. I managed to call 911 after that. The ambulance arrived and through my disorientation, I saw them take her down the narrow stairs on the gurney. I was uncontrollably stuck inside myself, unable to reflect, think, or react.

I sat there as he calmly stared at me. His story came in layers. He would peel back the layers, and as he peeled, it was like an onion until we reached the full magnitude of it all, bringing me to tears. I held back and swallowed the lump that formed in my throat.

Dale retold the story about how he had picked up his son late, and his ex called him stupid. He seethed about how she had called him names after bringing their son home later than usual. When he had written about it in the email, he hadn't gone into this much detail, only saying that he had blacked out. Now he elaborated that instead of him grabbing his keys and leaving, he blacked out and saw himself "choking the life out of her" and watching her die. The only thing that pulled him out of his trance was his son in the crib crying. When he snapped out of it, he grabbed his keys and went to a bar.

I remained motionless. He pressed on by asking, "Have you ever thought about killing someone?"

*What do I say to that?* "No." My body never moved. He was still looking at me with dead eyes.

"Well, if you did kill somebody, how would you do it?"

I felt like I was stuck in a bad horror flick. I needed processing time.

"Don't worry." He tried to console me. "I'm not gonna choke you tonight."

"That's not fucking funny at all."

"Yeah, poor timing."

My stomach was starting to turn, and I felt like I needed to poop, puke, and pass out. In my panic, I suggested we leave the beach and get back to the room. As we headed back to the car, I noticed his walk was unfamiliar and robotic. My system had been shocked and rebooted just to be shocked all over again. We both got into the car, and I retreated to my safe place—my mind. He tried holding my hand, but I wasn't feeling it. The gesture forced my mouth to find the words.

"I need to ask you a question."

"Yeah?"

"Are you suicidal?"

He laughed, which I did not find comforting, but I prepared myself for the answer.

"Well, if I told you that I was, I'd probably lose my job, because that's one of the things that I should not be. My friend who shot himself in the head knew all about this crazy world in my head. I understand why he thought that was his only way out."

I looked at him with great concern. "We need to call those therapists first thing Monday morning!"

# EXPOSED

We arrived at the quiet hotel. I could see how exhausted and depleted Dale was. We showered and went upstairs to eat. He ordered his usual New York strip and potatoes and kept poking at it with his fork and moving the mashed potatoes around. It was the first time I'd seen him not finish a meal. All he wanted to do was sleep. It seemed like he'd been holding this in for years. It seemed like he felt like he'd opened a can of worms with someone he felt safe with and was concerned how I would receive his darkest secret.

Dale's eyes and body were heavy. He said, "I can take a quick nap and be ready to go by eleven-thirty or midnight."

I told him, "I don't need to go out." I needed to process my feelings about our interactions, not a distraction.

I encouraged him to go back to the room to nap, and I went to hang out by the pool. *I wish I had a therapy appointment.* Unfortunately, I had recently lost my therapist and was trying to find a new one. I called my friend, Jade, to talk through everything. She was a good friend and a professional, and I could always count on her for good advice. I explained to her what went down—what he said and his demeanor.

"Coco, when did he get a divorce?" she asked.

"2013."

"Hmm... it sounds like he's still in a toxic and tumultuous environment. You've become his person and safe space. He's been holding that demon in for a long time."

She began talking about potential levels of personality disorder and some terms with which I was unfamiliar. I was listening, but I was still trying to move past frozen. Although the conversation was insightful, it did not help me process my emotions.

"Are you sure you want to stay? I'm not sure I want you to sleep in the room with him tonight," she said.

"He needs a therapist," I admitted.

"He needs more than that, maybe some schedule two meds. Are you *sure* he's divorced?"

"Yes, the divorce was finalized in 2013. There's no way he could still be in that environment. Maybe he just never fully processed the relationship." Nothing made any sense to me anymore. "We spend so much time together—it's just not possible. I think he's broken."

"Okay."

I could hear her trying to support me and detected the alarm in her voice. After we finished our talk, I sat by the pool a little longer, staring at the sky. I was so confused.

When I finally returned to the room, I found him passed out. That night, we had plans to meet up with the bartenders from the Signature Room after their shift. I wanted to let Dale sleep as much as he needed, but he popped up after hearing my phone. He was disoriented, but eager to go out.

I was okay with staying in for the night, but he insisted we head out. I held his face and said, "Are you doing this for me, or for you? I know you're exhausted, I'm fine to stay in."

He replied without hesitation, "Both of us!"

We did make it out to Club 939 with our favorite bartenders. We had a few cocktails with them and some enjoyable conversations.

The following morning Dale woke up first. I was on the other side of the bed, and he grabbed me and pulled me over to him to cuddle. "Assume your little spoon position," he joked. We lay in bed and watched some of the March Madness games.

"Stay with me... I want to grow old with you," he pleaded. "I'm calling every therapist on the list." He could sense my concern for his well-being and my concern about whether I had the energy or patience to stick this out. When he turned me over to face him, his eyes looked dejected.

◌

After we returned to our homes, he cried every time we spoke. I couldn't continue in his heaviness and wanted us to get to a better place. The relationship no longer felt light and hopeful. After several days, I had yet to fully process our night on the beach. Quickly returning to the realities of motherhood and work, I buried those experiences beneath my responsibilities as both an employee and a mother. I jumped back into the hectic schedule of dance classes, swimming lessons, hockey practice, flag football, grocery shopping, homework, cleaning the house, and the endless laundry.

I was still scared from the conversation on the beach. I kept rethinking and replaying—*did I miss something? How did I miss it? Was my fear valid? Was I overthinking?* I loved him. Love was blind, but the universe was trying to force me to see the red flags. Love kept me from deciding to break things off. I didn't want to move further until he had gotten to a space where he felt whole. He needed therapy, and I needed time. I didn't want to throw in the towel, but my feelings had shifted.

That week, Dale began his new assignment at the training facility for agents. The new role was more stable with less travel, which meant we were able to be more consistent. Though he lived in Virginia and I lived in Minnesota, he would be in Virginia more regularly now. On his first day on the job, he kept sending pictures of the facility and the exhibit wall while explaining certain things— like tiny details that wouldn't be seen by the naked eye but that the Secret Service agents were trained to see. He reminisced about his training days and seemed to feel like he was tapping into a new purpose. Subconsciously, I felt uncertain if I should stay invested.

My phone rang. It was Monique. She was concerned, like so many of my girlfriends were. I was just going through the motions, and everyone's alarms were going off. Monique asked for Dale's address. I gave it to her, and she said she would call me back later.

When she returned my call, she reminded me how I had researched through Google, Spokeo, and other online methods to profile him before we began dating. She told me that now she had gone further to find out about the current and previous owners of the property where he lived.

"Who is Paula Winthrop?" Monique asked.

"His ex-wife's name is Paula."

"Why is she on the deed and the loan to his house in Virginia?"

"What?"

"Yeah," Monique replied. "Dale and Paula are both on the deed and the loan to the house."

Monique told me they had purchased the house together in 2016, three years *after* the divorce. Dale had told me that he moved to Virginia the year after they divorced, in 2014. But this record showed them buying the house together after he claimed they had already divorced.

"But he's told me so many times that she's never been to Virginia," I said.

Monique was quiet.

Dale had told me that his ex was still in Detroit with their son. He told me his son would visit him during the summers, vacations, or whenever he had time off. Dale primarily went to Detroit because he traveled a lot for work; it made things easier to see his dad and his son.

I thought that maybe he had bad credit or something, which would explain why she was on the loan.

"Okay, um, figure it out, just call him right now." Monique's voice distracted me from my deep thoughts of forgiveness.

I called him. "Hey, babe. When was your divorce finalized?"

"2013. Why?"

"Remember when I asked you if your ex-wife had ever been to Virginia?"

"Yeah."

"What was your answer?"

"I said no, she's never been to Virginia. Why would she come here?" he asked.

"Okay, when was the last time your son was in Virginia."

"It's been like a year or so."

"Okay, Dale." At this point, I could not believe my own reservations. "I'm gonna ask you this question one last time, and I'm only asking you this because I believe I know the truth. Does your ex-wife live in Virginia?"

"Yes," he answered.

"Again, when was your divorce finalized?"

He hesitated. The truth would be spoken, so I silently waited for it.

"It's not," he confessed.

"Okay, walk me through this to help me understand. Is her maiden name Winthrop? And if yes, why is she on the deed to your house?"

He admitted his wife never took his last name, and things started coming together. For the first time in a long time, I felt like I had regained total control over all my faculties. I was able to self-reflect and analyze the situation. The questions began to pour from my mouth like water, and he answered them.

He admitted they bought the house together, which was why she was on the deed and loan. She was initially on the loan alone because they would split custody. Then they decided it might work out better if they were roommates. She had one master bedroom, and he had the other. They both dated other people; they planned to legally divorce after their son's high school graduation. He explained that they chose to delay the divorce because his son has a nonverbal learning disability, and they were worried he would regress.

"We knew something was off with him when he was five. He was diagnosed at seven when his teacher urged us to test him because he was so behind," he said. "He's likely not gonna go to college..."

If this was the case, though, why didn't he tell me that initially? And was I witnessing a grown man throw his son under the bus to support his lies? This was disturbing enough to push me from denial to anger, and it didn't even make sense.

"At the end of the day, if this is true, why wouldn't you give me the opportunity to decide for myself? You lied to me from the jump about everything. You *knew* my situation with my ex-boyfriend." Once those words poured from my mouth, I couldn't stop them. The more I talked, the more he cried, until he was crying like he had on the beach in Hawaii—an ugly, hyperventilating type of cry.

"Babe, I'm sorry," he pleaded with me, but I no longer had sympathy. My mind began to run through every memory of us from the beginning—every lie, every cover-up, and every dismissal.

"Babe, please. I promise you can call her and ask her this, and she'll tell you the same stuff," he begged.

He had duped me into falling for him. He had turned me into prey, and I was not okay with that. My anger turned to fury. My mouth became my protector. I was no one's victim. While screaming at him, I was texting my friend back and forth.

Monique suggested I call Paula, especially since he had told me to call her to confirm his story. I had to figure this out and get to the bottom of it once and for all. Dale began talking about how miserable his life was and how he felt suicidal, but my empathy was no longer available to him.

"You know what, I need *not* to talk to you anymore," I announced.

He continued to plead, but I was in disbelief.

The following morning, he called like he did every morning. I asked him, "Where did you sleep?"

He said, "The couch," which made no sense if they were just roommates and he had his own bedroom.

I had many more questions, but I wasn't confident I would receive straight answers from him. *Where does she sleep? Where's his wedding ring? Does she wear hers? Do you sit down as a family and eat?* My mind continued to race as he talked about how they were two ships passing in the night. He told me about his wife's job, and everything he mentioned aligned with what my friends had discovered.

Finally, after all his yammering, I decided to call her. "Fine, I'll call her to confirm what you're saying to me."

I hung up with him and called the number for his wife that he had given me, which matched what Monique had found online. She didn't answer. Afterward, I sent her a respectful text message:

> Hi, this is Coco. Dale and I have been in a relationship for the past nine months. It was my understanding that you divorced in 2013. Unfortunately, I just learned yesterday that that is, in fact, not the case. He explained to me that you guys are separated and plan to divorce after your son's graduation in 2024. This is all news to me. I am trying to understand the dynamics of your relationship. I would love to understand what's true and what's not true so that I can decide how to move forward. I'm open to speaking with you. I understand that this text message is probably not wanted, but again, I'm open to connecting.

I called him back and read the text message to him. He was calm, cool, and collected. He didn't even take a deep breath. He said, "I understand, babe. I recognize what I've done and own up to how much you hurt by my doing."

Thirty minutes later, he told me he had to answer because Paula was calling. He came back and told me how emotional she was and that he was going to finish the call with her. I was emotional and hurt by the whole thing and felt that it was best if I had time to myself.

Shortly after we hung up, Monique called to check in. I updated her on the latest, and she was in disbelief with some solid concerns. Things still weren't adding up. Why would a woman he had been separated from be emotional about my text unless he were still lying? Monique wanted me to dig deeper. Only the right questions would lead to the truths I desperately needed.

After ending his call with Paula, he called me back on his way home from work. Overcome with emotion, he pulled over to the side of the road, and we started a FaceTime conversation.

"I understand the disturbance of an unexpected text like this," I said, "but why would she be emotional and hurt if y'all are just roommates?"

"I guess she just didn't expect this to come, but you were part of my exit strategy," he replied.

"Bullshit!" It was more lies, and I was no longer drinking the Kool-Aid.

Dale finally told me that they were still married. She had had no idea that there was a divorce in the works. He kept telling me how she would joke around and say divorce often. He kept telling more lies to cover up the lies he had already told, and it became too much. I just wanted him to shut the fuck up.

"You are a whore!" I blurted out. "You've been out in these streets. Dating random ass women, lying... you're trash. You're the scum of the earth! Every day from the moment that I met you at Martha's Vineyard. The second that I grabbed your hand to see if you were married. You lied. You are a pro at this." I was fuming. I didn't know why I kept talking because nothing good would come of it—maybe I just needed to release. "Does she know about Lana, Madeline, Erica, and all these other women you've been with? Or Tisha, who texts you all the time? You're the devil in disguise. You ain't shit, and your homeboys... all of them knew. Y'all are all problematic."

"I don't want to lose you," Dale managed to say through his weeping.

"You already lost me!"

"You said you would be my friend if this didn't work out."

"That was clearly based on the premise that you were actually a decent fucking person. You are not. You are a predator!" I abruptly hung up on him. I couldn't stomach more deceit.

He called me back with a gun to his head, talking about killing himself.

"Take your anger out on me because I deserve it. I fucked up," he shouted.

I was stunned. "Nobody wants to be a punching bag. You just

want to use me to make yourself feel better about this whole situation. I made you feel good. That's why you used me, because I made you feel good. So if you're gonna kill yourself? Kill your fucking self. Don't kill your family. Don't come after me—kill yourself."

I was livid. He was at home, talking to me in the home he shared with Paula. I could hear her screaming in the background. He was crouched over and explaining the differences between me and her.

"She laughs about demeaning me and emasculating me, and all I can think about is that Coco would never call me stupid. You would never call me stupid." His voice sounded shaky and unstable, like a scolded child. I no longer wanted any part of this drama—whatever this was.

"Oh, you used me because I made you feel like a man. I made you feel like the top dog that you aren't. She probably made you feel emasculated because you are a child. Because you are a fucking bitch!" I hung up.

# FIVE DAYS

For five days, I did the bare minimum to show up as a mother, but I was a shell of myself. I didn't go to the gym or socialize. Once I got the kids on the bus, I turned off the lights and went back upstairs to my room. I was going through the motions of my work days but not accomplishing much. I attended meetings on my computer in my home office and took phone calls when needed. I rarely turned on my webcam, and if it was necessary, I threw on my glasses to distract from my appearance and sad eyes. I often got distracted on calls and needed extra coffee to help me focus. Words seemed to go in one ear and out the other.

I wasn't up to cooking anything complicated and had no appetite, so I used DoorDash for meals for the kids. Even throwing chicken nuggets or fries in the air fryer felt like so much effort. I barely slept.

I hadn't shared the situation with my mom or confided in my girlfriends. Only two friends knew about the initial discovery of Dale's lies. Monique and Jade knew parts, such as that Dale and Paula were both on the deed and loan to the house, but I hadn't followed up with them after confronting him with the details and learning more. They didn't know about our call when he had held himself at gunpoint. I went on silent autopilot, having not had a chance to process everything. I felt as if I were on an island all by myself, lost in my own thoughts.

My youngest son approached me and asked, "Mommy, are you okay?" His big brown eyes looked solemn.

"Yeah, why do you ask?"

"You seem sad. You look really sad." He had always been attuned to people's emotions.

I didn't want to lie to him. "I'm good. I'm going through some stuff, but I'll be good."

He gave me a hug, which helped in the moment but wasn't enough to pull me out of my fog.

Something Dale had said kept running through my mind. He called me his exit strategy, minimizing me to a plan when I had believed we had a future. He had gaslit and manipulated me for his own selfish purposes. I was just a tool for him to use when he felt bad.

Dale continued to call me until I blocked him by phone and on social media. The next day he sent me an email:

> *I fucked up and there's nothing I can do to take back what I did. What I'm going through is nothing compared to what I did to you. I was a horrible person to you. You're one of the nicest people I've ever met, and I'll never regret meeting you. Hopefully the wounds I've caused will heal in time. Again, I pushed you here, and I take full responsibility.*

Struggling with whether to respond, I had a glass of wine. My mind was still glitching as I tried to process my reality. *Thank goodness I never let him meet my kids.* In my mind, I revisited every event we had enjoyed together and reviewed my memories of all the days and nights he spent deceiving me, our fake conversations that served to connect us. I reflected on our closeness, our eye contact when I was being open and honest.

*What was wrong with me?* This internal war of reliving conversations felt like a scratched record playing the same few notes. *How did he do this? How did he have time? Where was she when I talked to him while he was home? Why had nothing jumped out at me?* My friends had tried to warn me, and I hadn't listened. *Had I done this to myself?*

I compulsively scrolled through our past messages, feeling detached, an audience member of my own life. I was trapped in a virtual reality or a scene from a horror film, not the existence I had envisioned for myself. Over and over, I reread our emails and poured over photos. *Was any of this real? Could it all be some elaborate prank? Was I merely dreaming?*

That weekend, the kids went to their father's. I still wasn't eating, but I drank more wine to dull the pain. I ended up drunk, incoherent, and unable to control the tears streaming down my face. Unprepared to discuss what I had uncovered, I kept ignoring all the calls and texts from my friends.

On Sunday night, I was so drunk I passed out. Then, in my inebriated state, I accidentally answered the phone when Stella called. She listened to my incoherent babble. "Okay, you wait right there for me. I'm coming over." She must have contacted my neighbor and friend, Regina, because they both showed up on my front porch. Their persistent shouts through a cracked window eventually reached me, as if I were in a dream. In my blurred state, I stumbled downstairs to open the front door.

My girls looked at me in astonishment. I dropped to my knees and sobbed uncontrollably, ugly cries with snot coming out of my nose as I wailed. They sat, listened to my blubbering, and held me, their silent support uplifting me. I cried so much that I began to hyperventilate. I had held it together well enough from a distance, but up close, I was like a hysterical baby.

The cry felt like it washed built-up toxins out of my body. I sobered up a bit and was able to tell them what had happened. They rubbed my back and exclaimed, "Fuck him!" at all the right points.

"Sweetheart, when was the last time you ate?" Stella asked.

I couldn't even remember. I had been on a liquid diet of wine since early that morning and hadn't had much actual food to eat the entire week, beyond nibbling a few french fries occasionally.

"I don't know," I responded so softly it was almost a whisper. I felt depleted, but for once, I did not feel alone. Stella began to prepare a turkey sandwich and Greek salad for me to eat.

It felt strange but relieving to eat. My girls made me smile and laugh, and my spirit lightened.

"Um, I don't mean to be rude," Regina interrupted, "but when was the last time you showered, my love?"

We all laughed. I hadn't showered all week and smelled ripe. As I went to shower and get dressed, Stella and Regina started to clean like little elves. They tidied up, put dishes in the dishwasher, gathered dirty laundry, and put kids' toys into the right bins. Like me, my house was in disarray.

I came down feeling more alive. The shower had cleaned my head, congested from all the crying, and my body felt clean.

When they were reassured that I was on better footing, they headed home.

"Girl, answer your phone next time. I will come and bust down this door if I have to," said Regina.

"Yes, ma'am!" I teased.

CB

I hated that even in all my turmoil, I still missed Dale. After Stella and Regina left, I began to think maybe he and his wife were separated. *How would that look if we continued?* I unblocked him. But I knew I was psyching myself out. I was riding a rollercoaster of emotions and playing the blame. My feelings were shaded by my past traumas and my childhood caused me to constantly second-guess myself.

My relationship with my dad played with my head. He had also done things that made me question what was real and what wasn't. When I was eighteen, I got home one day to him holding a credit card in my name. He said I could have it if I paid off $1500 of his bills. The limit was $5000, so I agreed, thinking it was $3500 of free money. Later I realized that he must have used my social security number to apply for a credit card, and then manipulated me into paying his overdue bills.

I've had a history of being snowed by men with empty words and promises. I remembered Dale's curiosity to learn every detail of how I had uncovered that my ex was married. He had been sitting on the edge of his seat, eagerly asking follow-up questions. I had shared everything with Dale, hoping it would build an understanding between us, but instead, it became the blueprint he used to manipulate and deceive me.

I'm not usually a Taylor Swift fan, but I was playing my Spotify, and her song, "My Tears Ricochet" came on. It smacked me upside the head. I listened to that song on repeat. It helped lift me out of my darkness and put me in a different head space.

The music helped me tap into my emotions I had suppressed for the first few days. In my relationship with Dale, I had tried to assert myself and be clear about my boundaries, but I hadn't enforced them. I couldn't let someone else's faults tear me apart, nor could I continue to move the same ways through the world and expect different results. My job was to care for myself, not for him. A real man doesn't need a job description, blueprint, or lies to win over a woman. I didn't deserve all the hell he gave me.

I sent an email to his boss about my concern over his thoughts of killing his wife and his suicidal behavior. I'd met him several times on trips to Hawaii, and Dale had shared several emails from his boss when he was complaining about the watch and being reprimanded for casual attire, so I had his direct contact information.

*Hi Mark,*

*It's Koryeah. We met a few times in Hawaii. Unfortunately, I am writing to you based on concern for the safety of Dale, his family, and myself. I recently learned that he is still married despite telling me that he was divorced in 2013. When I asked him about this, he put a gun to his head and threatened to kill himself and his wife. Dale has had some mental health struggles that I believe the agency has been unaware of. I have tried to help him get professional help, but he has not acted on the resources I've shared with him to my knowledge. Please let me know if I can answer any questions you may have.*

*Koryeah*

# THE INTERVIEW

M ark responded right away and asked for a meeting. I asked a couple of my friends who were attorneys, "Do I need to have an attorney present?" They said no, and advised I just focus on telling the truth and letting them draw their own conclusion based on the facts I shared. They said that if I was ever uncomfortable or pressured, I should speak up or leave the meeting.

"This is strictly about him," the agent confirmed. "We just want to understand the situation."

Basically, Dale was under investigation, not me. Still, Regina said she was coming to Starbucks to sit with me as support.

I was supposed to meet them at 9:30 a.m. I drank coffee, trying not to work myself up too much before the interview. Coffee sometimes helps to get my brain going. This morning, my stomach was doing all types of cartwheels, and I had diarrhea from the stress.

When I arrived a few minutes late, Regina was already there waiting. Across the room were the two agents at another table. We approached them together and sat down.

The woman was blonde, and the man had dark hair. Both wore

typical Secret Service black suits. The woman offered to grab my drink, but I went to get it myself, a stall tactic to give myself time to gain more composure before I sat to talk with them.

The agents didn't seem overly friendly but didn't pressure me. Two colleagues joined them on a video call on a laptop. They prefaced the meeting by restating their concern about their agent, but they were also concerned for the safety of his wife, child, and me as well. Their main objective in understanding our situation was to protect the Obamas. My task was to walk them through our entire relationship. They wanted to know how exactly we met and what took place in those nine months.

They seemed concerned about the email that I had sent them about Dale's suicidal and homicidal thoughts. They needed to know if he shared any privileged information about former presidents and vice presidents, or political information. They also asked for copies of pictures and text sent between us. As I retold our story, reliving certain moments brought me to tears. They realized that not only had Dale shared photos of the Obamas' house, but he had also brought me there. I told them he had asked me to go, even though I didn't want to.

"Why did you go?" the woman agent asked.

"Honestly, I went because he wanted me to. There was a constant push from him to know about his life as an agent. His identity and self-esteem seemed to be based solely on his job. I don't believe he had anything else."

"Have you really been there?" the woman agent followed up.

"I know you can check the security cams. You know I've been there."

"Well, can you describe it to me?"

I started explaining the place to them and gave them a verbal tour. The man agent looked at me with an expression that confirmed he believed me, nodding to his online colleague.

"Have *you* been there?" I asked the woman agent.

"No, I haven't."

I described the entire encounter at the house and how Dale had hidden me in the bathroom when other people had arrived.

"Did you guys do anything in the house?"

"No, why?" She was referring to Michelle's bathroom and how Dale tried to convince me to have sex there.

"What if we go back and look at the tapes?"

"Then you're not gonna see anything because we didn't have sex in there. Anyway, there aren't cameras in her bathroom."

"How do you know that?"

"Dale shared everything and laid out the entire setup. The bathroom has no cameras. Why would there be cameras in her bathroom anyway?"

I also showed them photos on my phone to corroborate what I was saying.

"What do you plan on doing with those photos?"

"Nothing. I'm not going to send them to *TMZ* or anything like that."

"Well, we aren't trying to make you delete the photos unless there's a larger investigation. Can you please send us the pictures via email after this meeting?" They also requested I send anything else he shared with me. I scrolled through my pictures of Alicia Keys' house, Steven Spielberg's boats, Melinda Gates, Tyler Perry, and Amal Clooney.

"Do you know why he did this?"

"I don't know. Like I told you before, there was nothing else to him. I didn't ask him for them and don't care about them. These were things that mattered to him. He would send these pictures to me unprompted."

"He was really oversharing," the female agent remarked.

He had done plenty of things that he should not have. Dale would tell me when and where the Obamas were in Aspen or where the girls were going during that same time. I knew their code names. I knew what day Orange Theory was, what day she had private tennis lessons, and when her personal trainer came. He would even take videos of Michelle and send them to me. I knew where they were and what restaurants they ate at. I knew who was in town, for how long, and where they departed to go next. Then, after sharing, he would send me pictures.

The meeting was intense and lasted nearly four hours. I was exhausted afterward. They were alarmed by the amount of information he had readily shared with me.

"Our job, first and foremost, is our protectees. We need to ensure they aren't in jeopardy. He shared information that could put them at risk." They also expressed concern for my safety based on everything I shared about his mental health and the escalation of events a week prior.

"Your first line of defense is to call your local police. And do you have a conceal carry license?" the male agent asked.

I confirmed, "Yes, I have protection."

"Your second, if needed, is to get a restraining order. You can always reach out to us if you need anything, or for concerns, but we can't be here as fast as the local police can."

The conversation confirmed to me that he was dangerous, and I needed to strictly keep my distance from him.

The agents thanked me for my time and headed to the airport. I gave Regina a hug and thanked her for being there to support me.

&#x43;&#x42;

Poison doesn't necessarily always present itself outright. The Secret Services process includes extensive screenings for agents—drug tests, security clearance, medical exams, credit checks, and polygraph exams—but they clearly missed something with Dale. When we first started dating, he informed me that he had to go back once or twice for a polygraph exam because they were stuck on one question: How many times had he smoked weed in his life? He was adamant about it being twice, and according to him, they wanted to dig more into the fact that he kept saying it was only two times. Ultimately, he passed and got the job.

Sometimes, it takes the effects to realize what you have been ingesting. I didn't need them to tell me I was in danger. It helped me to know that I wasn't losing my mind. My gut had been speaking to me all along, but I didn't listen until it screamed loud and clear, both inside and out. I needed to focus on the whispers more.

# HEALING

Six weeks later, my cousins and I hopped on a plane to Miami for Afro Nation to dance, laugh, and vibe with our people. I was hoping it would miraculously jumpstart my healing, make me forget Dale, and allow me to forgive myself so that I could move on. I couldn't have asked for a better artist lineup. The concerts were at night, though, and by the end of the day, I didn't want to be around a bunch of people. Even though I'd flown to Miami just for the concert, I didn't go—I just sat in my hotel room, feeling empty and watching TV.

It really hit me when my birthday came around and I didn't want to do anything. Knowing I was a big celebration person, everyone was calling to find out what kind of extravaganza I planned. I didn't have any. I had stressed myself into feeling sick the week of my birthday and used that as an excuse to not do anything.

I made plans with friends and then canceled. I stayed home, crying from watching commercials or listening to song lyrics. I binged in the evenings, even ordering McDonald's—a fast food chain I hadn't indulged in for over two decades. Trapped in a persistent low mood, I felt myself spiraling and was uncertain how to break the cycle.

Dale's deception messed with my head. I went through my phone and deleted his pictures, but those Google memories irked my soul. A picture would pop up in my feed, and I would have the same visceral response. I questioned myself—*why did I keep going back? Why didn't I follow my instincts?*

CB

My girlfriend, Crystyn, asked me to join her on a trip to Malta. I wasn't sure I was ready for international travel, but I decided to push myself.

While there, we talked so much about life, relationships, divorce, motherhood, etc. I needed her energy, optimism, and no-bullshit outlook on life. We laughed, I cried, and she helped me get to a better place of letting go of self-blame about my relationship with Dale. She had recently returned from a week at a Black-centered healing retreat called Mwasi in Marrakech, Morocco, and introduced me to the owner, Tanesha Barnes.

Once I returned home from Malta, I still had the travel itch, and while communicating with Tanesha, I learned more about the Mwasi Global Community in Marrakech.

One month later, I made the trek to Marrakech. There was always a sense of peace that filled me when I set foot on the continent of Africa. Mama Africa reminded me to pause, reset, rejoice, embrace, be still, and remember who I was and where I came from.

My time at the Mwasi retreat resuscitated me in a way that was different from therapy and formal treatments. There was a soul, an energy, a smell of the air that instantly brought about this feeling of peace, grounding, and connectivity. It was a feeling I realized that I have always sought in relationships, but I failed to realize that I could find it within myself.

Much like my trip to Martha's Vineyard a year earlier, in Morocco, I slowed down without distractions. My time there forced me to feel all the feelings, and in return, I refueled my soul, smile, and zest for life. I confronted so much on this trip, leaving my pain in the desert. I remembered to pause, breathe, tap into my most powerful self, and live the life I deserve. I found my confidence and came home ready to face and embrace myself.